D1709047

Beginning Svelte

Greg Lim – Daniel Correa

FIRST EDITION: JULY 2022

CO-AUTHOR: DANIEL CORREA

Table of Contents

PREFACE

About this book

In this book, we take you on a fun, hands-on and pragmatic journey to quickly learn Svelte and get familiar with how it works. You'll start building Svelte apps within minutes. Every section is written in a bite-sized manner and straight to the point as we don't want to waste your time (and most certainly ours) on the content you don't need. In the end, you will have what it takes to develop a real-life app.

Requirements

Basic familiarity with HTML, CSS, Javascript and object-oriented programming. No prior knowledge of Svelte is required as we start from basics.

Contact and Code Examples

The source codes used in this book can be obtained by emailing support@i-ducate.com.

Send any comments or questions concerning this book to https://twitter.com/greglim81 or email support@i-ducate.com.

CHAPTER 1: INTRODUCTION

What is Svelte?

Svelte is a frontend, open-source JavaScript framework to make interactive web pages. It is similar to other frontends frameworks such as React, Vue, Angular where you create reusable UI components to build interactive user interfaces.

But the difference is that Svelte compiles application code into optimized JavaScript at *build time*. Frameworks like React in contrast interpret code at *runtime*. React interprets code at runtime and generates a virtual representation of the UI (virtual DOM) in memory. It looks at the difference between the virtual and the actual DOM, and syncs both of them by updating the actual DOM. So, there is a performance cost behind the framework's abstractions.

Why use Svelte?

Because there is no virtual DOM in Svelte and application code is compiled into highly optimized JavaScript code, Svelte becomes more lightweight and performs faster than other frameworks. User experience is also smoother and faster.

Svelte is also easier to learn than other frameworks like React. Most of the things that are complicated with other frameworks (e.g. managing state) are simple with Svelte. You can do a lot more with less code.

Svelte like other frameworks, allow you to create dynamic frontend UIs, and also provide great animations/transitions that are easy to use.

Step by Step

I will teach you about Svelte from scratch in step by step fashion. You will build an application where you can input search terms and receive the search results via GitHub RESTful API (fig. 1).

Figure 1

In the end, you will also build a real-world ToDo application with full C.R.U.D. operations (fig. 2).

To Do	Date Created	Complete	Edit	Delete
Buy Dinner	Mon Apr 11 2022	Mark Complete	Edit	Delete

Completed Todos

To Do	Date Created	Complete	Delete
Fetch Kid from Tuition	Tue Apr 12 2022	Mark Uncomplete	Delete
Post on twitter.com/greglim81	Tue Apr 12 2022	Mark Uncomplete	Delete

Figure 2

These are the patterns you see on a lot of real-world applications. In this book, you will learn how to implement these patterns with Svelte.

Thinking in Components

A Svelte app is made up of reusable components. For example, if we want to build a storefront module like what we see on Amazon, we can divide it into three components. The search bar component, sidebar component and products component.

Components can also contain other components. For example, in *products* component where we display a list of products, we do so using multiple *product* components. Also, in each *product* component, we can have a *rating* component (fig. 3).

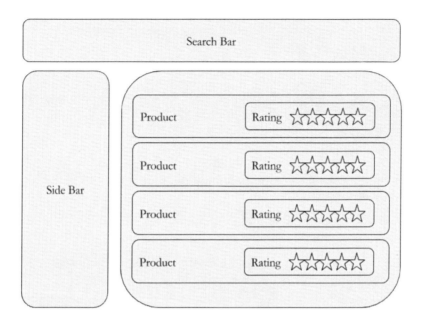

Figure 3

The benefit of such an architecture helps us to break up a large application into smaller manageable components. Plus, we can reuse components within the application or even in a different application. For example, we can re-use the rating component in a different application.

A Svelte component self-contains content (HTML markup), behavior (JavaScript) and the presentation (CSS) in a *.svelte* file. Below is an example of a product component that displays a simple string containing the product name:

Analyze Code

```
<script>
  let name = 'bag';
</script>

<h1>The product name is {name}!</h1>

<style>
  h1{
    color: blue;
  }
<style>
```

Components have their logic placed in <script> tags. Using JavaScript, you can set values for variables, create functions to control the HTML output etc. In the example, we declared a *name* variable which we refer in the markup: `<h1>The product name is {name}!</h1>`.

This outputs the HTML "The product name is bag".

In the curly braces, you can put any JavaScript code, e.g. variables, expressions, conditionals, loops (as we shall see later).

You specify the CSS you want to apply in the <style> tag.

This is the big picture of thinking in terms of components. As you progress through this book, you will see more of this in action.

Setting Up

Installing Node

First, we need to install NodeJS. NodeJS is a server-side language and we don't need it because we are not writing any server-side code. We mostly need it because of its *npm* or Node Package Manager. *npm* is very popular for managing dependencies of your applications. We will use *npm* to install other later tools that we need.

Get the latest version of NodeJS from *nodejs.org* and install it on your machine. Installing NodeJS should be pretty easy and straightforward.

To check if Node has been properly installed, type the below on your command line (Command Prompt on Windows or Terminal on Mac):

Execute in Terminal

```
node -v
```

and you should see the node version displayed.

To see if npm is installed, type the below on your command line:

Execute in Terminal

```
npm -v
```

and you should see the npm version displayed.

Using Degit to Create a New Project

The easiest way to start a Svelte project is to use *vite*, a project scaffolding tool. In the Terminal, run the command:

Execute in Terminal

```
npm init vite firstapp
```

Then, you will be asked some questions. Follow the next instructions:
- "Need to install the following packages: create-vite". Type 'y', and press 'Enter'. This will only appear if you had not installed this package before.
- "Select a framework". Select 'svelte', and press 'Enter'.
- "Select a variant". Select 'svelte', and press 'Enter'.

This will download a Svelte project template to a newly created *firstapp* folder. Next, run the following:

Execute in Terminal

```
cd firstapp
npm install
npm run dev
```

This creates a new project in the firstapp directory, installs its dependencies (we look at them later) and start a server on http://localhost:3000 (fig. 4).

Figure 4

If you point your browser to localhost:3000, you will see the "Hello World" example running (fig. 5):

11

Figure 5

Project File Review

Now let's look at the project files with a code editor. In this book, we will be using VScode (https://code.visualstudio.com/) which is a good, lightweight and cross-platform editor from Microsoft. If you are using VSCode, install the 'Svelte for VS Code' extension (fig. 6).

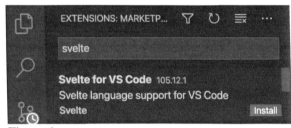

Figure 6

This gives you formatting, auto-complete and allows you to use *emmet* (helps write HTML fast) within Svelte components.

When you open the project folder in VScode editor, you will find a couple of files (fig. 7).

Figure 7

We will not go through all the files as our focus is to get started with our first Svelte app quickly, but we will briefly go through some of the more important files and folders.

Our app lives in the *src* folder. All Svelte components go here. Any other files outside of this folder are meant to support building your app. In the course of this book, you will come to appreciate the uses for the rest of the library files and folders.

In the *src* folder, we have *main.js* which is the entry point for our app where we initialize and bring in the main App component:

Analyze Code

```
import App from './App.svelte'

const app = new App({
  target: document.getElementById('app')
})

export default app
```

App.svelte

App component is defined in src/App.svelte:

Analyze Code

```
<script>
  import logo from './assets/svelte.png'
  import Counter from './lib/Counter.svelte'
```

13

```
</script>

<main>
  <img src={logo} alt="Svelte Logo" />
  <h1>Hello world!</h1>

  <Counter />

  <p>
    Visit <a href="https://svelte.dev">svelte.dev</a> to learn how to
build Svelte
    apps.
  </p>

  <p>
    Check out <a
href="https://github.com/sveltejs/kit#readme">SvelteKit</a> for
    the officially supported framework, also powered by Vite!
  </p>
</main>

<style>
  :root {
    font-family: -apple-system, BlinkMacSystemFont, 'Segoe UI', Roboto,
Oxygen,
      Ubuntu, Cantarell, 'Open Sans', 'Helvetica Neue', sans-serif;
  }

  …

</style>
```

package.json

package.json is the node package configuration which lists the packages our project uses. For example, in *devDependencies*, it is using the Svelte 3.* framework and the 'vite' module as indicated in **bold**:

Analyze Code
```
…
  "devDependencies": {
    "@sveltejs/vite-plugin-svelte": "^1.0.0-next.30",
    "svelte": "^3.44.0",
    "vite": "^2.9.9"
  }
}
```

Under *scripts*, we have the *build* command (*npm run build*) to compile our Svelte code into optimized

14

JavaScript for production.

Analyze Code

```
...
  "scripts": {
    "dev": "vite",
    "build": "vite build",
    "preview": "vite preview"
  },
...
```

We also have the *dev* command to start our dev server with live reload. i.e. Svelte auto-detects code changes and the app reloads automatically with the revised code so you don't have to refresh the page every time your code changes.

index.html

The root folder contains index.html which is our Single Page Application that is loaded in the browser:

Analyze Code

```
<!DOCTYPE html>
<html lang="en">
  <head>
    <meta charset="UTF-8" />
    <link rel="icon" href="/favicon.ico" />
    <meta name="viewport" content="width=device-width, initial-scale=1.0"
/>
    <title>Svelte + Vite App</title>
  </head>
  <body>
    <div id="app"></div>
    <script type="module" src="/src/main.js"></script>
  </body>
</html>
```

In *<div id="app"></div>* the App.svelte component code will be injected.

Summary

In this chapter, we were introduced to Svelte, a simple and lightweight JavaScript framework which compiles code into optimized JavaScript to make dynamic frontend UIs. We set up the environment (using Vite) to begin developing Svelte apps and reviewed the purpose of certain files in a Svelte project. In the next chapter, we will continue to see how to create and use Svelte components.

CHAPTER 2: CREATING AND USING COMPONENTS

In the previous chapter, you learned about the core building blocks of Svelte apps, components. In this chapter, we will implement a custom component from scratch to have an idea of what it is like to build a Svelte app.

Creating our First Component

In VScode, open the project folder that you have created in chapter 1. In *src*, create a new folder *components* to store all our components (fig. 1).

Figure 1

In *components*, create a new file *Products.svelte* (fig. 1).

Note the naming convention of the file; we capitalize the first letter of the component *Products* followed by *.svelte*.

Type out the below code into *Products.svelte*:

Add Code

```
<script>
</script>

<h1>Products</h1>
```

Our Products component simply outputs the string 'Products'.

Importing and Using our Created Component

A component can be used by other components. Let's import and add *<Products />* to src/App.svelte. Remove the existing codes in src/App.svelte and place it with the below:

Replace Entire Code

```
<script>
    import Products from './components/Products.svelte';
</script>

<main>
    <Products />
</main>
```

Code Explanation

We first import *Products* component into *App* component using *import*:

Analyze Code

```
<script>
    import Products from './components/Products.svelte'
</script>
```

For custom components we have defined, we need to specify their path in the file system. Because Products Component is in the *components* folder, we import from '.' /components/Products.svelte'.

The path is relative to the current component path. './' means same folder. You will use '../' to go back one folder and so on.

We have just referred to the Products component from App component. We can also render *Products* multiple times. Modify the App.svelte with the following in **bold**:

Modify Bold Code

```
...
<main>
    <Products />
    <Products />
    <Products />
</main>
```

Now save the file and go to your browser. You should see the Products component markup displayed with the message (fig. 2):

18

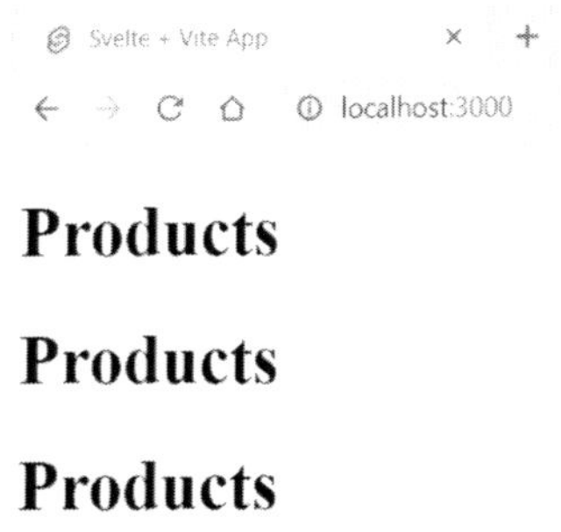

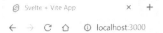

Svelte + Vite App
localhost:3000
Products
Products
Products

Figure 2

Embedding JavaScript Expressions

You can embed JavaScript expressions in your markup by wrapping them in curly braces. For example, we can define functions, properties and render them in the output. The below has a function *formatName* which takes in a *user* object with *firstName* and *lastName* properties. We then call *formatName* in curly braces.

Analyze Code

```
<script>
	const user = {
		firstName:'Greg',
		lastName:'Lim'
	};

	function formatName(user){
		return user.firstName + ' ' + user.lastName;
	}
</script>

<h1>Hello {formatName(user)}</h1>
```

You can also use curly braces to embed a JavaScript expression in an attribute for example:

Analyze Code

```
<script>
	const user = {
		firstName:'Gressg',
		lastName:'Lim',
		imageUrl:'https://picsum.photos/200/300'
	};
</script>

<img src={user.imageUrl} alt="sample" />
```

Displaying a List with Loops

We will illustrate displaying a list of products with loops in *Products*. In src/components/Products.svelte, add the codes shown in **bold** below:

Modify Bold Code

```
<script>
    let products = [
        {
            id: "1",
            name: "airpods"
        },
        {
            id: "2",
            name: "kindle"
        },
        {
            id: "3",
            name: "keyboard"
        }
    ];
</script>

<h1>Products</h1>
{#each products as product (product.id)}
      <h3>{product.id}: {product.name}</h3>
{/each}
```

Back in src/App.svelte, render the Products component one time with the following in **bold**:

Modify Bold Code

```
<script>
      import Products from './components/Products.svelte'
</script>

<main>
      <Products />
      <Products />
      <Products />
</main>
```

Navigate to your browser and you should see the result in fig. 3

Products

1: airpods

2: kindle

3: keyboard

Figure 3

Code Explanation

Analyze Code

```
<script>
    let products = [
        {
            id: "1",
            name: "airpods"
        },
        ...
    ];
```

First, in <script> of *Products component*, we declare an array *products* which contain the id and names of products.

Analyze Code

```
{#each products as product (product.id)}
    <h3>{product.id}: {product.name}</h3>
{/each}
```

We next use the {*#each*}{*/each*} block to loop through each element in *products*. For each element, we output:

Analyze Code

```
<h3>{product.id}: {product.name}</h3>
```

Note that we have provided a *key* attribute (*product.id*) for our product items. The key (product.id) tells Svelte how to figure out which DOM node to change when *products* update. Thus, when dynamically editing the list, and removing/adding elements, you should always pass an identifier in lists to prevent issues.

Summary

You have learned a lot in this chapter. If you get stuck while following the code or if you would like to get the sample code we have used in this chapter, contact me at support@i-ducate.com.

In this chapter, we created our first custom component. We created a Products Component that retrieves product data from an array and renders that data (using the *#each* loop) on the page. In the next chapter, we will explore props, state and events in Svelte.

CHAPTER 3: SVELTESTRAP, PROPS, STATE AND EVENTS

In this chapter, we will explore displaying data by binding controls in a HTML template to properties of a Svelte component, how to apply CSS classes on styles dynamically, how to use the component state and how to handle events raised from DOM elements.

Using SvelteStrap

We will be using SvelteStrap to make our UI look more professional. SvelteStrap (https://sveltestrap.js.org/) is a library of reusable front-end components (like forms, buttons, icons) similar to Bootstrap to help build user interfaces for Svelte applications.

Installing SvelteStrap

Go to the *firstapp* directory in the Terminal and run:

Execute in Terminal
```
npm install sveltestrap svelte
```

Next, in the existing project from chapter two, we need to reference *bootstrap.css*. Go to 'sveltestrap.js.org'. Under 'Get Started', copy the stylesheet link (fig. 1):

Adding Bootstrap

Sveltestrap does not include or embed Bootstrap CSS so this needs to be installed by you, either by including Bootstrap CSS to your layout (1) , or installed from npm (2).

1. Include in layout

Either static HTML layout

Figure 1

and add it to <head> of *index.html* with the following in **bold**:

Modify Bold Code

```
<!DOCTYPE html>
<html lang="en">
  <head>
    <meta charset="UTF-8" />
    <link rel="icon" href="/favicon.ico" />
    <meta name="viewport" content="width=device-width, initial-scale=1.0"
/>
    <title>Svelte + Vite App</title>
    <link rel="stylesheet"
href="https://cdn.jsdelivr.net/npm/bootstrap@5.1.0/dist/css/bootstrap.min
.css">
  </head>
  <body>
    <div id="app"></div>
    <script type="module" src="/src/main.js"></script>
  </body>
</html>
```

To check if we have installed SvelteStrap correctly, add a button into src/App.svelte by adding the lines in **bold**:

Modify Bold Code

```
<script>
    import { Button } from 'sveltestrap';
    import Products from './components/Products.svelte';
</script>

<main>
    <Products />
    <Button color='primary'>Click Me</Button>
</main>
```

If you have successfully linked to SvelteStrap, you should get your button displayed like in fig. 2.

Products

1: airpods

2: kindle

3: keyboard

Click Me

Figure 2

There are times when we want to use different CSS classes on an element. For example, if we add the 'danger' button style as shown below:

Analyze Code
```
<Button color='danger'>Click Me</Button>
```

we get the below button style (fig. 3).

Products

1: airpods

2: kindle

3: keyboard

Figure 3

And if I want to disable the button by applying the *disabled* class, I can do the following

Analyze Code
```
<Button color='primary' disabled>Click Me</Button>
```

More information of styles of *button* and other components are available at the SvelteStrap site under 'Components' (fig. 4).

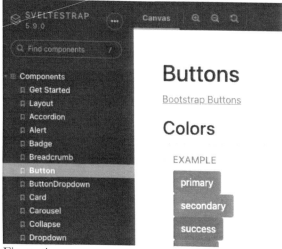

Figure 4

Disabling Button on Condition

Now, suppose I want to disable the button based on some condition. We can do the below:

```
                        Analyze Code
<script>
     import { Button } from 'sveltestrap';
     import Products from './components/Products.svelte'

     let isValid = true;
</script>
<main>
     <Products />
     <Button color='primary' disabled={!isValid}>Click Me</Button>
</main>
```

That is, when *isValid = false* the *disabled* CSS class will be applied, making the button unclickable. If *isValid = true* the *disabled* CSS class will not be applied, making the button clickable.

Props

We can pass data into a component by using 'props'. For example, suppose we want to display a list of products with its rating. We will need to pass the rating value to our rating component. We can do something like: *<Rating rating="4"/>* to display a rating of 4 stars.

To do so, in *src/components*, create a new file Rating.svelte. Next, our Rating component needs to export the *rating* prop. Fill in the below codes:

26

Add Code
```
<script>
    export let rating = 0;
</script>

<h1>Rating: {rating}</h1>
```

By exporting, we expose the prop to parent components. When a parent component renders *<Rating rating="4"/>*, the *rating* attribute will contain the value of 4. We then render the rating value in <main>.

In *src/App.svelte,* replace the previous code with the following:

Replace Entire Code
```
<script>
    import Rating from './components/Rating.svelte';
</script>

<main>
    <Rating rating='1' />
    <Rating rating='2' />
    <Rating rating='3' />
    <Rating rating='4' />
    <Rating rating='5' />
</main>
```

If you run your app, it should display something like:

Rating: 1
Rating: 2
Rating: 3
Rating: 4
Rating: 5

Figure 5

In App.svelte, we first have *<Rating rating="1"/>*. Svelte calls the Rating component with *rating:*

27

'*1*' as the props. Our Rating component outputs a `<h1>Rating: 1</h1>` as the result.

In this example, we pass in only one attribute as props. We can pass multiple attributes and even complex objects as props. We will illustrate this later in the book.

Improving the Look

We will improve the look of our rating component by showing rating stars like what we see on Amazon.com instead of showing the rating value numerically. A user can click select from a rating of one star to five stars. We will implement this as a component and reuse it in many places. For now, don't worry about calling a server or any other logic. We just want to implement the UI first.

To show rating stars instead of just number values, we will use the Icon component (fig. 5) from *https://sveltestrap.js.org/?path=/story/components--icon* which provides popular icons in our Svelte project.

Icons

Bootstrap Icons

EXAMPLE

Hello 🌐!

```
<script lang="ts">
  import { Icon } from 'sveltestrap';
</script>

<h1>
  Hello <Icon name="globe2" />!
</h1>
```

Figure 6

Note: To use the icon component, we need to include a link to Bootstrap Icon CSS (fig. 6):

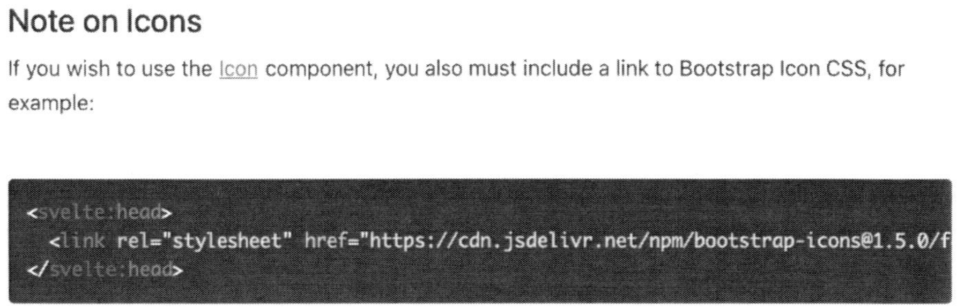

Note on Icons

If you wish to use the Icon component, you also must include a link to Bootstrap Icon CSS, for example:

```
<svelte:head>
  <link rel="stylesheet" href="https://cdn.jsdelivr.net/npm/bootstrap-icons@1.5.0/f
</svelte:head>
```

Figure 7

Thus, in index.html, add:

Modify Bold Code

```
<!DOCTYPE html>
<html lang="en">
  <head>
    <meta charset="UTF-8" />
    <link rel="icon" href="/favicon.ico" />
    <meta name="viewport" content="width=device-width, initial-scale=1.0"
/>
    <title>Svelte + Vite App</title>
    <link rel="stylesheet"
href="https://cdn.jsdelivr.net/npm/bootstrap@5.1.0/dist/css/bootstrap.min
.css">
    <link rel="stylesheet" href="https://cdn.jsdelivr.net/npm/bootstrap-
icons@1.5.0/font/bootstrap-icons.css">
  </head>
  <body>
    <div id="app"></div>
    <script type="module" src="/src/main.js"></script>
  </body>
</html>
```

We will be using the *star* and *star-fill* icons (fig. 7):

Figure 8

To include them in our project, add the below codes in **bold** into Rating component:

Modify Bold Code

```
<script>
    import { Icon } from 'sveltestrap';

    export let rating = 0;
</script>

<h1>Rating: {rating}</h1>
{#if rating >= 1}
    <Icon name="star-fill" />
{:else}
```

```
    <Icon name="star" />
{/if}
{#if rating >= 2}
    <Icon name="star-fill" />
{:else}
    <Icon name="star" />
{/if}
{#if rating >= 3}
    <Icon name="star-fill" />
{:else}
    <Icon name="star" />
{/if}
{#if rating >= 4}
    <Icon name="star-fill" />
{:else}
    <Icon name="star" />
{/if}
{#if rating >= 5}
    <Icon name="star-fill" />
{:else}
    <Icon name="star" />
{/if}
```

Code Explanation

We first import *Icon* from SvelteStrap with

Analyze Code
```
<script>
    import { Icon } from 'sveltestrap';
```

We then render the *star* and *star-fill* icons with:

Analyze Code
```
{#if rating >= 1}
    <Icon name="star-fill" />
{:else}
    <Icon name="star" />
{/if}
```

Conditional Rendering

We conditionally render a filled star if *rating is >= 1*. Else, render a normal (empty) star.
There is an opening {#*if*} and an ending {/*if*}. The opening markup checks for a value or statement
(e.g. *rating* >= 1) to be true.

The above code is for the first star. The remaining similar repetitions are for the four remaining stars. However, note the change in value of each condition depending on which star it is. For example, the second star's condition should be

Analyze Code

```
{#if rating >= 2}
    <Icon name="star-fill" />
{:else}
    <Icon name="star" />
{/if}
```

The second star should be empty if the rating is less than two. It should be filled if the rating is more than or equal to two. The same goes for the third, fourth and fifth star.

We revisit If-Else conditional code in chapter 5.

Running your App

When we run our app, we get the icons displayed:

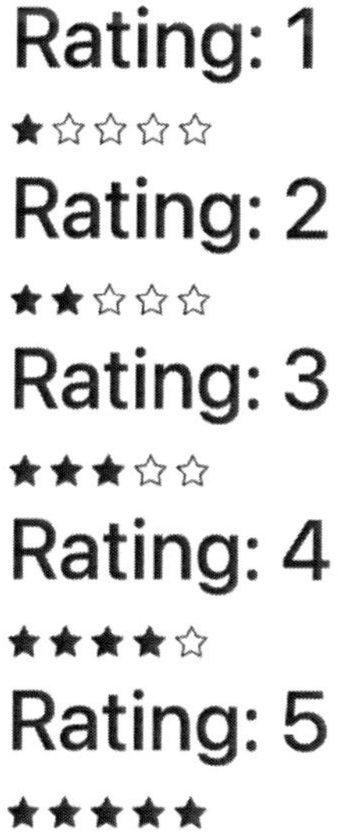

Rating: 1

★☆☆☆☆

Rating: 2

★★☆☆☆

Rating: 3

★★★☆☆

Rating: 4

★★★★☆

Rating: 5

★★★★★

Figure 9

State in a Svelte Component

Every component in addition to having its own markup, CSS and JavaScript logic, can host its own state in <script>. Rating component has its state variable *rating* in <script>:

Analyze Code

```
<script>
    import { Icon } from 'sveltestrap';

    export let rating = 0;
</script>
```

State manages data that will change within a component. Whenever state changes, the UI is re-rendered to reflect those changes. We often refer to this as the component or local state.

If you come from other frameworks like Vue or React, you might ask, "how do I update the state?" For example, in React, you might have to use things like *setState* or use the *useState* hook which makes it rather unintuitive.

A great thing about Svelte is that we don't need to do anything special to update the state of a component. We simply assign a new value to it with the = operator, e.g. *rating = 2, rating = rating + 1*

Now, suppose we want our user to be able to change the rating by clicking on the specified star. How do we make our rating component render in response to a user click?

Handling Events

Next, we want to assign a rating depending on which star the user has clicked. To do so, our component needs to handle the click event. In Svelte, you can define a listener for a DOM event in the template using the *on: <event>* syntax.

For example, to make our rating component handle user clicks, we pass a function to the *on:click* attribute:

Modify Bold Code

```
...

<h1>Rating: {rating}</h1>
<span on:click={() => rating = 1}>
{#if rating >= 1}
    <Icon name="star-fill" />
{:else}
    <Icon name="star" />
{/if}
</span>
<span on:click={() => rating = 2}>
{#if rating >= 2}
```

32

```
      <Icon name="star-fill" />
{:else}
      <Icon name="star" />
{/if}
</span>
<span on:click={() => rating = 3}>
{#if rating >= 3}
      <Icon name="star-fill" />
{:else}
      <Icon name="star" />
{/if}
</span>
<span on:click={() => rating = 4}>
{#if rating >= 4}
      <Icon name="star-fill" />
{:else}
      <Icon name="star" />
{/if}
</span>
<span on:click={() => rating = 5}>
{#if rating >= 5}
      <Icon name="star-fill" />
{:else}
      <Icon name="star" />
{/if}
</span>
```

We wrap each star's *if-else* clause in a *span* element and pass in an arrow function as the event handler to the *click* event.

For example, we have: `<span on:click={() => rating = 1}>` to assign a rating of one if a user clicks on this star.

We then change the value of the argument to the arrow function depending on which star it is. The second star's *on:click* should be `<span on:click={() => rating = 2}>`.

So, when a user clicks on the second star, *rating* is assigned with value of two. When a user clicks on the third star, *rating* is assigned value of three and so on.

Note that whenever a state variable has a new value assigned to it, our component automatically re-renders thus showing the updated value on to the view.

Running your App

When you run your app now, you should be able to see your ratings and also adjust their values by clicking on the specified star.

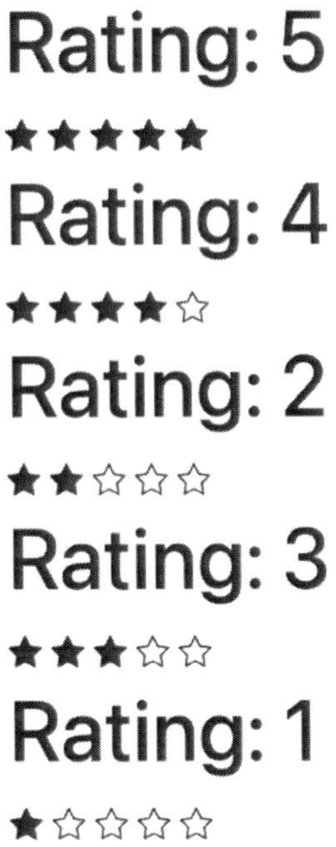

Rating: 5

★ ★ ★ ★ ★

Rating: 4

★ ★ ★ ★ ☆

Rating: 2

★ ★ ☆ ☆ ☆

Rating: 3

★ ★ ★ ☆ ☆

Rating: 1

★ ☆ ☆ ☆ ☆

Figure 10

Note that we have five different rating components each having their own local state. Each updates independently. Each rating component does not affect another rating component's state.

Summary

In this chapter, we learned about binding controls in a HTML template to Svelte component properties, using the component state and handling events raised from DOM elements. We used SvelteStrap to make our UI more professional. In the next chapter, we will see how to put multiple components together in an application.

Contact me at support@i-ducate.com for the full source code of this chapter or if you encounter any errors with your code.

CHAPTER 4: WORKING WITH COMPONENTS

In this chapter, we will learn more about using components, how to reuse them and put them together in an application. Execute the codes in the following sections in your existing project from chapter three.

Styles

We can further modify our components with our own CSS styles. These *styles* are scoped only to your component. They won't effect to the outer DOM or other components.

To illustrate, suppose we want our filled stars to be orange, in src/components/Rating.svelte we add the following in **bold**:

<code>Modify Bold Code</code>

```
<script>
    import { Icon } from 'sveltestrap';

    export let rating = 0;
    let color = 'orange';
</script>

...
```

We create a new state variable *color* to contain the style color. If required, you can further specify other styling properties like *height*, *backgroundColor*, *fontSize* etc.

To apply this style, add the below *style* attribute:

<code>Modify Bold Code</code>

```
...

<h1>Rating: {rating}</h1>
<span style="color:{color}" on:click={() => rating = 1}>
{#if rating >= 1}
    <Icon name="star-fill" />
{:else}
    <Icon name="star" />
{/if}
</span>
...
```

Do the same for the rest of the stars. When we run our application, we will see our filled stars with the orange CSS applied to it (fig. 1).

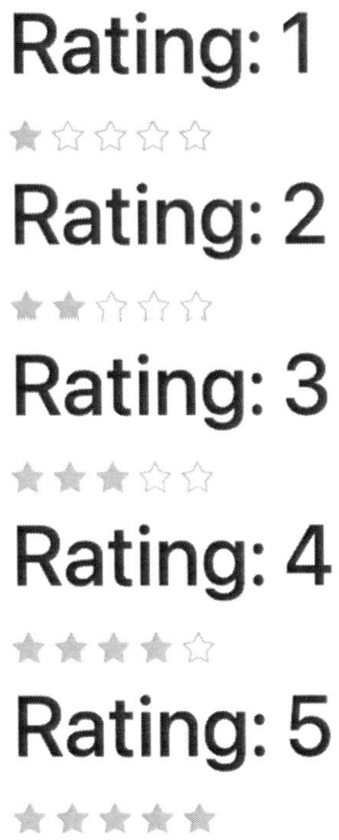

Rating: 1

★☆☆☆☆

Rating: 2

★★☆☆☆

Rating: 3

★★★☆☆

Rating: 4

★★★★☆

Rating: 5

★★★★★

Figure 1

And if we re-assign blue to *color*,

Analyze Code

```
<script>
    import { Icon } from 'sveltestrap';

    export let rating = 0;
    let color = 'blue';
</script>
```

...

We get:

Rating: 1

★ ☆ ☆ ☆ ☆

Rating: 2

★ ★ ☆ ☆ ☆

Rating: 3

★ ★ ★ ☆ ☆

Rating: 4

★ ★ ★ ★ ☆

Rating: 5

★ ★ ★ ★ ★

Figure 2

4.2 Example Application

We will reuse the rating component that we have made and implement a product listing like in figure 3.

Products

Product 1
May 31, 2016
★ ★ ★ ★ ☆ 2
Lorem ipsum dolor sit amet, consectetur adipiscing elit. Aenean porttitor, tellus laoreet venenatis facil
sit amet mauris.

Product 2
October 31, 2016
★ ★ ☆ ☆ ☆ 12
Lorem ipsum dolor sit amet, consectetur adipiscing elit. Aenean porttitor, tellus laoreet venenatis facil
sit amet mauris.

Figure 3

This is like the list of products on Amazon. For each product, we have an image, the product name, the product release date, the rating component and the number of ratings it has.

In *src/components*, create a new component file *Product.svelte* that contains the Product Component. This component will be used to render one product. Now, how do we get our template to render each product listing like in figure 2? We use the *Card* component in SvelteStrap. Go to *sveltestrap.js.org/?path=/story/components—card* (fig. 4).

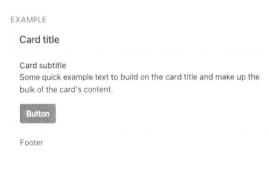

Figure 4

Copy the below slightly modified and simplified markup into *Product.svelte* (check that it is *Product.svelte* and not *Products.svelte*) markup:

Add Code

```
<script>
    import Rating from './Rating.svelte';
    import {
      Image,
      Card,
      CardTitle,
      CardBody,
      CardSubtitle,
      CardText
    } from 'sveltestrap';

    export let data = {
        imageUrl: "",
        productName: "",
        releasedDate: "",
        rating: 0,
        numOfReviews: 0,
        description:""
    };
</script>

<Card class="mb-3">
    <CardBody>
        <Image thumbnail alt="Landscape" src={data.imageUrl} />
        <CardTitle>{data.productName}</CardTitle>
        <CardSubtitle>{data.releasedDate}</CardSubtitle>
        <Rating rating={data.rating} numOfReviews={data.numOfReviews} />
        <CardText>
            {data.description}
        </CardText>
    </CardBody>
</Card>
```

Code Explanation

We first import *Rating* component and *Card* related components.

Next, in the markup, notice that to assign values of our product, we used props to inject the values (indicated in **bold**). Our Product component is expecting a *props data* object with the fields: *imageUrl*, *productName*, *releasedDate*, *description*, *rating* and *numOfReviews*.

We have also added our rating component that expects input rating and number of reviews.

Analyze Code

```
<Rating rating={data.rating} numOfReviews={data.numOfReviews} />
```

numOfReviews prop

Our rating component currently only has *rating* as input. Add the *numOfReviews* prop in the *Rating* component and remove the *h1* tag:

Modify Bold Code

```
<script>
    import { Icon } from 'sveltestrap';

    export let rating = 0;
    export let numOfReviews = 0;
    let color = 'orange';
</script>

<h1>Rating: {rating}</h1>
...
```

And display the number of reviews beside the rating stars:

Modify Bold Code

```
...
<span style="color:{color}" on:click={() => rating = 5}>
{#if rating >= 5}
    <Icon name="star-fill" />
{:else}
    <Icon name="star" />
{/if}
{numOfReviews}
</span>
```

Products.svelte

Next in *src/components/Products.svelte*, declare a *products* array that contains a list of products. Type in the below code (or copy it from the source code) into *Products.svelte*.

Replace Entire Code

```
<script>
    import Product from './Product.svelte';

    let products = [
        {
```

40

```
        id: '1',
          imageUrl: "http://loremflickr.com/150/150?random=1",
          productName: "Product 1",
          releasedDate: "May 31, 2016",
          description: "Lorem ipsum dolor sit amet, consectetur..",
          rating: 4,
          numOfReviews: 2
      },
      {
        id: '2',
          imageUrl: "http://loremflickr.com/150/150?random=2",
          productName: "Product 2",
          releasedDate: "October 31, 2016",
          description: "Lorem ipsum dolor sit amet, consectetur..",
          rating: 2,
          numOfReviews: 12
      },
      {
        id: '3',
          imageUrl: "http://loremflickr.com/150/150?random=3",
          productName: "Product 3",
          releasedDate: "July 30, 2016",
          description: "Lorem ipsum dolor sit amet, consectetur..",
          rating: 5,
          numOfReviews: 2
      }
    ];
</script>

<h1>Products</h1>
{#each products as product}
    <Product data={product} />
{/each}
```

Notice that in our component, we currently hardcode an array of product objects. Later on, we will explore how to receive data from a server.

For *imageUrl*, we use http://loremflickr.com/150/150?random=1 to render a random image 150 pixels by 150 pixels. For multiple product images, we change the query string parameter *random=2, 3,4* and so on to get a different random image.

The code in *<main>* is similar to the one in chapter three where we loop through the names in *products* array to list them. This time however, our element is not just simple strings but a *data* object which contains Product properties *imageUrl, productName, releasedDate, description, rating* and *numOfReviews*.

Lastly in *src/App.svelte*, make sure you import and render your *Products* component:

Replace Entire Code

```
<script>
    import Products from './components/Products.svelte';
</script>

<main>
    <Products />
</main>
```

Save all your files and you should have your application running fine like in figure 5.

Products

Product 1

May 31, 2016

★ ★ ★ ★ ☆ 2

Lorem ipsum dolor sit amet, consectetur adipiscing elit. Aenean porttitor, tellus laoreet venenatis facil sit amet mauris.

Product 2

October 31, 2016

★ ★ ☆ ☆ ☆ 12

Lorem ipsum dolor sit amet, consectetur adipiscing elit. Aenean porttitor, tellus laoreet venenatis facil sit amet mauris.

Figure 5

Summary

In this chapter, we illustrate how to modify CSS styles taken from SvelteStrap and reusing components to put them together in our example Product Listing application.

Contact me at support@i-ducate.com if you encounter any issues or for the full source code of this chapter.

CHAPTER 5: CONDITIONAL RENDERING

In this chapter, we will explore functionality to give us more control in rendering HTML via JSX.

5.1 If-Else

Suppose you want to show or hide part of a view depending on some condition. For example, we have earlier displayed our list of products. But if there are no products to display, we want to display a message like "No products to display" on the page. To do so, in src/components/Products.svelte of the existing project from chapter four, add the codes in **bold**:

Modify Bold Code

```
...

<h1>Products</h1>
{#if products.length > 0}
    {#each products as product}
        <Product data={product} />
    {/each}
{:else}
    No products to display
{/if}
```

Now when we rerun our app, we should see the products displayed as same as before. But if we comment out our hard-coded data in Products.svelte and return an empty array instead, we should get the following message.

Products

No products to display

Figure 1

Code Explanation

Analyze Code

```
{#if products.length > 0}
    {#each products as product}
        <Product data={product} />
    {/each}
```

We use the opening {#if} to check if *listProducts.length > 0*. If the condition is true, i.e. *listProducts.length >*

0 is true, the element right after {#if} will appear in the output. If it is false, Svelte will ignore and skip it.

Analyze Code

```
{:else}
    No products to display
{/if}
```

Otherwise (else) show what follows {:else} which is `No products to display`. We have actually previously used this to conditionally render either a filled star or an empty one.

5.2 *Slots*

Sometimes, we need to insert content into our component from the outside. For example, we want to implement a component that wraps a bootstrap jumbotron. A bootstrap jumbotron (fig. 2) as defined on getbootstrap.com is "A lightweight, flexible component that can optionally extend the entire viewport to showcase key content on your site."

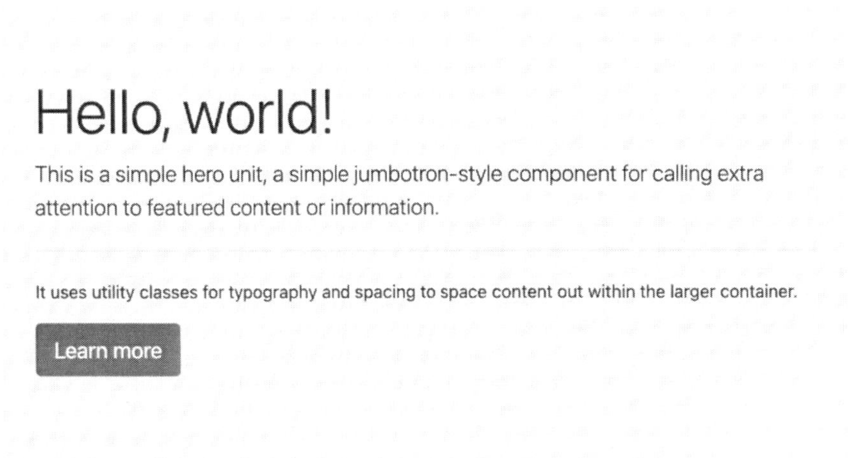

Hello, world!

This is a simple hero unit, a simple jumbotron-style component for calling extra attention to featured content or information.

It uses utility classes for typography and spacing to space content out within the larger container.

Learn more

Figure 2

Here is an implementation of the bootstrap jumbotron component (create a new file JumboTron.svelte in src/components).

Add Code

```
<script>
    import { Button, Jumbotron } from 'sveltestrap';
</script>

<Jumbotron>
    <h1 class="display-3">Hello, world!</h1>
```

```
    <p class="lead">
        This is a simple hero unit, a simple Jumbotron-style component
for calling
        extra attention to featured content or information.
    </p>
    <hr class="my-2" />
    <p>
        It uses utility classes for typography and spacing to space
content out
        within the larger container.
    </p>
    <p class="lead">
        <Button color="primary">Learn More</Button>
    </p>
</Jumbotron>
```

The markup above can be obtained from:
https://sveltestrap.js.org/v4/?path=/story/components--jumbotron

The Jumbotron component is called in *src/App.svelte* using (replace the previous code with the following),

Replace Entire Code
```
<script>
    import JumboTron from './components/JumboTron.svelte';
</script>

<main>
    <JumboTron />
</main>
```

To supply content to the jumbotron component, we can use *attributes* like:

Analyze Code
```
<JumboTron body='…' />
```

This is not ideal however. For we probably want to write a lengthier markup here like,

Analyze Code
```
<JumboTron>
    This is a long sentence, and I want to insert content into the
    jumbotron component from the outside.
</JumboTron>
```

That is to say, we want to insert content into the jumbotron component from the outside. To do so, we use *slots* as shown below (modify **bold** code in JumboTron.svelte):

Modify Bold Code

```
<script>
    import { Button, Jumbotron } from 'sveltestrap';
</script>

<Jumbotron>
    <h1>Hello, world!</h1>
    <p><slot></slot></p>
    <p><Button>Learn more</Button></p>
</Jumbotron>
```

In the code above, *<slot></slot>* will be the string between *<JumboTron>* and *</JumboTron>*. E.g.

App.svelte

Modify Bold Code

```
<script>
    import JumboTron from './components/JumboTron.svelte';
</script>

<main>
    <JumboTron>
        This is a long sentence, and I want to insert content into the
        jumbotron component from the outside.
    </JumboTron>
</main>
```

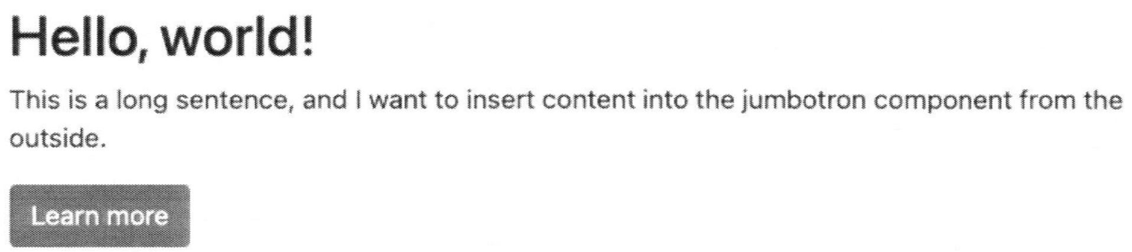

Hello, world!

This is a long sentence, and I want to insert content into the jumbotron component from the outside.

Figure 3

Summary

In this chapter, we explored {#*if*} {*:else*} that gives us more conditional control in rendering our template. We have also learned about inserting content into components from the outside using *Slots*.

Contact me at support@i-ducate.com if you encounter any issues or for the source code of *Product.svelte* and *Jumbotron.svelte*.

CHAPTER 6: BUILDING FORMS

In this chapter, we look at how to implement forms with validation logic in Svelte. As an example, we will implement a login form that takes in fields *email* and *password*.

Cloning the firstapp project

We are going to work on the development of a different application. So, you must duplicate the *firstapp* folder and call the duplicated folder *formsapp* (which is the folder that we will use across this chapter). Or you can work in your existing project from chapter 5.

Create an Initial Form Template

First, in *src/components* folder create a new file *UserForm.svelte* and copy-paste the form template from SvelteStrap (https://sveltestrap.js.org/?path=/story/components--formgroup) into it:

Add Code

```
<script>
    import { Badge, Form, FormGroup, Input, Label } from 'sveltestrap';
</script>

<Form>
    <FormGroup floating label="Floating Label">
        <Input placeholder="Enter a value" />
    </FormGroup>

    <FormGroup floating>
        <Input placeholder="Enter a value" />
        <div slot="label">
            Floating Label Slot <Badge>3</Badge>
        </div>
    </FormGroup>
</Form>
```

We then make some changes to the form:

Modify Bold Code

```
<script>
    import { Button, Form, FormGroup, Input, Label } from 'sveltestrap';
</script>

<Form>
```

49

```
<FormGroup floating label="Enter email">
    <Input type="email" />
</FormGroup>

<FormGroup floating label="password">
    <Input type="password" />
</FormGroup>

<Button type="submit" color="primary">Submit</Button>
</Form>
```

Code Explanation

Analyze Code

```
<script>
    import { Button, Form, FormGroup, Input, Label } from 'sveltestrap';
</script>
```

First, we import the *Form* and *Button* SvelteStrap components that will be used.

We convert both inputs into an email and password input. We changed the type of the email input to 'email' and type of the password input to 'password'. Lastly, we added a 'Submit' button.

Analyze Code

```
<Form>
    <FormGroup floating label="Enter email">
        <Input type="email" />
    </FormGroup>

    <FormGroup floating label="password">
        <Input type="password" />
    </FormGroup>

    <Button type="submit" color="primary">Submit</Button>
</Form>
```

Note, under *<Form>*, we have a *<FormGroup>* component which wraps a *<Input>* component. This renders an *input* (or *textarea/select* component if specified) with bootstrap styling. *FormGroup* provides *input* with proper spacing, along with support for a label (fig. 1).

50

Figure 1

The form provides some default email validation upon submission of the form, for e.g it has to include an '@'. We will later see how to add our own custom validation like whether it contains spaces and display alerts if the form fields have not been filled in correctly.

Running the Form

We can try running the form by rendering UserForm in App.svelte:

Replace Entire Code

```
<script>
    import UserForm from './components/UserForm.svelte';
</script>

<main>
    <UserForm />
</main>
```

And it should look something like:

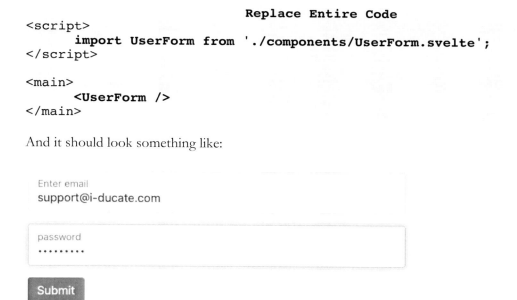

Figure 2

Handling Inputs with Bindings

In most Svelte apps, it's convenient to have a JavaScript function that handles the submission of the form and has access to the data that the user entered into the form. This is done by storing these user-entered data in the component state. In src/components/UserForm.svelte, add in the below two lines in **bold**:

Modify Bold Code

```
<script>
    import { Button, Form, FormGroup, Input } from 'sveltestrap';
    let email = '';
    let password = '';
</script>

...
```

We declare two state variables *email* and *password* and set their initial value to an empty string "". Next, add the below to the markup:

Modify Bold Code

```
...

<Form>
    <FormGroup floating label="Enter email">
        <Input type="email" bind:value={email} />
    </FormGroup>

    <FormGroup floating label="password">
        <Input type="password" bind:value={password} />
    </FormGroup>

    <Button type="submit" color="primary">Submit</Button>
</Form>

<p class="p-3 mt-3 border">
    Email: {email}
    <br>
    Password: {password}
</p>
```

Code Explanation

To bind *email* in the component state to the email form field, we have *bind:value={email}*. This creates a two-way binding between the data and the UI. If *email* changes, the input field will update its value. The opposite is true as well. If the form is updated by the user, the *email* variable value changes. The same applies for *password*: *bind:value={password}*

We illustrate this by displaying the values below the form by adding:

Analyze Code

```
...
</Form>

<p class="p-3 mt-3 border">
    Email: {email}
    <br>
    Password: {password}
</p>
```

When we run the app, we should see the values displayed at the bottom of the form like:

Figure 3

* Note that *email* and *password* variable must be defined with *let/var* and not *const*. *const* defines a variable with a value that can't change.

Showing Specific Validation Errors

Currently, we have the default email validation. But we should be able to have specific validation errors depending on the input given, for example "Email is required", or "Email should be a minimum of six characters" and show corresponding validation error alerts when a user submits the form.

To show specific validation errors, we declare two state variables to store our email and password error messages, and two Booleans to state if email and password fields are valid. Add the following code:

Modify Bold Code

```
<script>
    import { Button, Form, FormGroup, Input } from 'sveltestrap';
    let email = '';
    let password = '';
    let emailMessage = '';
    let passwordMessage = '';
```

```
    let validEmail = false;
    let validPassword = false;
</script>
```

...

To handle form submission, we define a *handleSubmit* handling function. We then bind *handleSubmit* to the *onSubmit* event handler in the *Form* element:

Modify Bold Code

```
<script>
    import { Button, Form, FormGroup, Input } from 'sveltestrap';
    let email = '';
    let password = '';
    let emailMessage = '';
    let passwordMessage = '';
    let validEmail = false;
    let validPassword = false;

    const handleSubmit = event => {
        event.preventDefault();
        if(validEmail){
            alert('Email: ' + email + '\nPassword: ' + password);
        }
    };
</script>

<Form on:submit={handleSubmit}>
...
```

So, when the form is submitted, *handleSubmit* will be called.

Svelte passes *event* as the argument of the function which is useful if we need to reference the *Event* object e.g. `preventDefault()` (to ensure the page isn't reloaded when we send the contents of the form).

In a normal app, we will want to send the form to some external API e.g. login. But before we send the network request, in *handleSubmit*, we want to perform some client-side validation. For example, if *username* length is zero, if it's less than a minimum length, if there are spaces in between etc. We first illustrate this for the email field by adding a *handleEmailInput* function:

Modify Bold Code

```
<script>
    ...

    const handleSubmit = event => {
        event.preventDefault();
        handleEmailInput();
        if(validEmail){
            alert('Email: ' + email + '\nPassword: ' + password);
        }
    };

    const handleEmailInput = () => {
        validEmail = false;
        if(email.length < 6){
            emailMessage = "Email should be minimum 6 characters";
        }
        else if(email.indexOf(' ') >= 0){
            emailMessage = 'Email cannot contain spaces';
        }
        else{
            emailMessage = '';
            validEmail = true;
        }
    };
</script>

...
```

In *handleEmailInput*, for each *if*-clause, we check for a specific validation, and if so, assign the specific error message to *emailMessage*. Only when it manages to reach the last *else* clause that we know we have no email validation errors and we set the boolean *validEmail* to true and *emailMessage* to an empty string.

And if *validEmail* is true, we then show an alert with what has been entered into the form.

Running your App

Now when you run your app, fill in a valid email and click on submit, an alert box appears with the inputted values (fig. 4).

Figure 4

Let's repeat the above steps for the password field. We add a *handlePasswordInput* function similar to *handleEmailInput*:

Modify Bold Code

```
<script>
    …

    const handlePasswordInput = () => {
        validPassword = false;
        if(password.length < 6){
            passwordMessage = "Password should be minimum 6 characters";
        }
        else if(password.indexOf(' ') >= 0){
            passwordMessage = "Password cannot contain spaces";
        }
        else{
            passwordMessage = '';
            validPassword = true;
        }
    };
</script>
```

…

And in *handleSubmit*, we add the check for a valid password as well:

Modify Bold Code

```
<script>
    …



    const handleSubmit = event => {
        event.preventDefault();
        handleEmailInput();
        handlePasswordInput();
        if(validEmail && validPassword){
            alert('Email: ' + email + '\nPassword: ' + password);
        }
    };


    …
</script>
```

…

When you run your app now, the submission will only be successful when both email and password fields have valid values.

In a normal app, instead of showing an alert, we will usually send the data in a request to some API. We will illustrate this in a later chapter.

Showing Validation Error Messages

Now, if we enter an invalid email address or password, our form doesn't submit because of the validation checks we have added in. But we should be showing validation errors to the user for her to correct her input as well. We will do that in this section.

First, import the *Alert* component from SvelteStrap:
(https://sveltestrap.js.org/?path=/story/components--alert):

Modify Bold Code

```
<script>
    import { Alert, Button, Form, FormGroup, Input } from 'sveltestrap';
    …
```

Alerts provide feedback messages for user actions. We add the *Alert* below our email and password input fields:

Modify Bold Code

...

```
<Form on:submit={handleSubmit}>
    <FormGroup floating label="Enter email">
        <Input type="email" bind:value={email} />
    </FormGroup>

    {#if emailMessage.length > 0}
        <Alert color="danger">
            {emailMessage}
        </Alert>
    {/if}

    <FormGroup floating label="password">
        <Input type="password" bind:value={password} />
    </FormGroup>

    {#if passwordMessage.length > 0}
        <Alert color="danger">
            {passwordMessage}
        </Alert>
    {/if}

    <Button type="submit" color="primary">Submit</Button>
</Form>
```

...

We wrap a condition around the *<Alert>*. We show the error message only if the error message's length is more than 0, indicating that there is an error.

So, if we run our app now, and submit with an email that is less than 6 characters and a password with spaces we get (fig. 5):

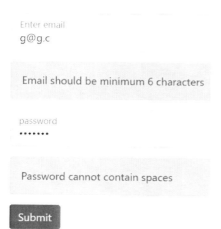

Figure 5

So, you see how you can extend your application with more validation checks?

Clearing the Fields Upon Successful Submit

Currently, after submitting our forms, the user-entered values in the fields remain. They should be cleared out after submission. To do so, in *handleSubmit*, after successful validation, we clear the *email* and *password* state and also set validEmail and validPassword to false:

Modify Bold Code

```
<script>
    ...

    const handleSubmit = event => {
        event.preventDefault();
        handleEmailInput();
        handlePasswordInput();
        if(validEmail && validPassword){
            alert('Email: ' + email + '\nPassword: ' + password);
            email = "";
            password = "";
            validEmail = false;
            validPassword = false;
        }
    };

    ...
```

Now, when you run your app again and submit the form, because the field values are binded to the state's,

59

the fields will be cleared out.

Exercise

Note that we have completed our login form, try to come up with your own form and have additional inputs like text-areas, check boxes, radio buttons and more. The markup for them is available at *https://sveltestrap.js.org/?path=/story/components--inputs*. They all work similar to the input fields that we have gone through.

Complete Code

We have covered a lot about Svelte Forms in this chapter. Below lists the complete code for *UserForm.js* which is also available in my source code.

Analyze Code

```
<script>
    import { Alert, Button, Form, FormGroup, Input } from 'sveltestrap';
    let email = '';
    let password = '';
    let emailMessage = '';
    let passwordMessage = '';
    let validEmail = false;
    let validPassword = false;

    const handleSubmit = event => {
        event.preventDefault();
        handleEmailInput();
        handlePasswordInput();
        if(validEmail && validPassword){
            alert('Email: ' + email + '\nPassword: ' + password);
            email = "";
            password = "";
            validEmail = false;
            validPassword = false;
        }
    };

    const handleEmailInput = () => {
        validEmail = false;
        if(email.length < 6){
            emailMessage = "Email should be minimum 6 characters";
        }
        else if(email.indexOf(' ') >= 0){
            emailMessage = 'Email cannot contain spaces';
        }
```

```
            else{
                emailMessage = '';
                validEmail = true;
            }
        }

    const handlePasswordInput = () => {
        validPassword = false;
        if(password.length < 6){
            passwordMessage = "Password should be minimum 6 characters";
        }
        else if(password.indexOf(' ') >= 0){
            passwordMessage = "Password cannot contain spaces";
        }
        else{
            passwordMessage = '';
            validPassword = true;
        }
    }
</script>

<Form on:submit={handleSubmit}>
    <FormGroup floating label="Enter email">
        <Input type="email" bind:value={email} />
    </FormGroup>

    {#if emailMessage.length > 0}
        <Alert color="danger">
            {emailMessage}
        </Alert>
    {/if}

    <FormGroup floating label="password">
        <Input type="password" bind:value={password} />
    </FormGroup>

    {#if passwordMessage.length > 0}
        <Alert color="danger">
            {passwordMessage}
        </Alert>
    {/if}

    <Button type="submit" color="primary">Submit</Button>
</Form>

<p class="p-3 mt-3 border">
    Email: {email}
    <br>
```

61

```
    Password: {password}
</p>
```

Summary

In this chapter, we learnt how to create a form with validation logic. We created an initial form with template from *SvelteStrap*. We learned how to use *bind:value* to bind component state variables to form fields. We used JavaScript functions to handle form submission.

We show form specific form field validation errors and how to validate the form upon submission.

Now after submitting a form, we need to persist the data by calling the API endpoint of the server. We will begin to explore how to communicate with the server in a later chapter.

Contact support@i-ducate.com if you have not already had the full source code for this chapter.

CHAPTER 7: GETTING DATA FROM RESTFUL APIS

In this chapter, we will see how to call backend services to get data through RESTful APIs with the Axios library.

Cloning the formsapp project

We are going to work on the development of a different application. So, you must duplicate the *formsapp* folder and call the duplicated folder *apiapp* (which is the folder that we will use across this chapter). Or you can work in your existing project from chapter 6.

GitHub RESTful API

Building RESTful APIs is beyond the scope of Svelte because Svelte is a client-side technology whereas building RESTful APIs require server-side technology like NodeJS, Django, ASP.NET, and so on. (I have written books on NodeJS and Django. Contact support@i-ducate.com if you are interested).

We will illustrate by connecting to the GitHub RESTful API to retrieve and manage GitHub content. You can know more about the GitHub API at

```
https://developer.github.com/v3/
```

But as a quick introduction, we can get GitHub users data with the following url,

```
https://api.github.com/search/users?q=<search term>
```

We simply specify our search term in the url to get GitHub data for user with name matching our search term. An example is shown below with search term *greg*.

```
https://api.github.com/search/users?q=greg
```

When we make a call to this url, we will get the following JSON objects as a result (fig. 1).

```
{
  "total_count": 37894,
  "incomplete_results": false,
  "items": [
    {
      "login": "greg",
      "id": 1658846,
      "node_id": "MDQ6VXNlcjE2NTg4NDY=",
      "avatar_url": "https://avatars.githubusercontent.com/u/1658846?v=4",
      "gravatar_id": "",
      "url": "https://api.github.com/users/greg",
      "html_url": "https://github.com/greg",
      "followers_url": "https://api.github.com/users/greg/followers",
      "following_url": "https://api.github.com/users/greg/following{/other_user}",
      "gists_url": "https://api.github.com/users/greg/gists{/gist_id}",
      "starred_url": "https://api.github.com/users/greg/starred{/owner}{/repo}",
      "subscriptions_url": "https://api.github.com/users/greg/subscriptions",
      "organizations_url": "https://api.github.com/users/greg/orgs",
      "repos_url": "https://api.github.com/users/greg/repos",
      "events_url": "https://api.github.com/users/greg/events{/privacy}",
      "received_events_url": "https://api.github.com/users/greg/received_events",
      "type": "User",
      "site_admin": false,
      "score": 1.0
    },
    {
      "login": "gregkh",
      "id": 14953,
      "node_id": "MDQ6VXNlcjE0OTUz",
      "avatar_url": "https://avatars.githubusercontent.com/u/14953?v=4",
      "gravatar_id": "",
      "url": "https://api.github.com/users/gregkh",
      "html_url": "https://github.com/gregkh",
      "followers_url": "https://api.github.com/users/gregkh/followers",
      "following_url": "https://api.github.com/users/gregkh/following{/other_user}",
      "gists_url": "https://api.github.com/users/gregkh/gists{/gist_id}",
      "starred_url": "https://api.github.com/users/gregkh/starred{/owner}{/repo}",
      "subscriptions_url": "https://api.github.com/users/gregkh/subscriptions",
      "organizations_url": "https://api.github.com/users/gregkh/orgs",
      "repos_url": "https://api.github.com/users/gregkh/repos",
      "events_url": "https://api.github.com/users/gregkh/events{/privacy}",
      "received_events_url": "https://api.github.com/users/gregkh/received_events",
      "type": "User",
      "site_admin": false,
      "score": 1.0
    },
```

Figure 1

Getting Data

To get data using a RESTful API, we are going to use the Axios library. Axios is a promise-based HTTP client for the browser and Node.js. We use it to make ajax calls to the server.

Axios provides the *get()* method for getting a resource, *post()* for creating it, *patch()* for updating it, *delete()* for delete and *head()* for getting metadata regarding a resource. We will illustrate using Axios to get data from a RESTful API in the following code example. In chapter nine, we will illustrate using axios for post, patch and delete as well.

To begin, in *src/components* folder, create a new file GitHub.svelte with the below code.

Add Code

```
<script>
import { onMount } from 'svelte';
import axios from 'axios';

onMount(async () => {
    try {
        const res = await axios.get(
            'https://api.github.com/search/users?q=greg'
        );
        console.log(res.data.items);
    } catch (e) {
    }
});
</script>
```

Code Explanation

The code in *onMount* will return GitHub data from our API endpoint. We will later explain what's *onMount*, but we first dwell into the code inside *onMount*.

To call our API endpoint, we need to use the *axios* library. First, install *axios* by executing the following in Terminal:

Execute in Terminal

```
npm install axios
```

Then in GitHub.svelte, import it using

Analyze Code

```
import axios from 'axios';
```

In *axios.get*, we call the GitHub API with argument 'greg'.

Analyze Code

```
    const res = await axios.get(
        'https://api.github.com/search/users?q=greg'
    );
```

axios.get returns a Promise which we subscribe to using *async/await* so that the code reads like synchronous code:

Analyze Code

```
onMount(async () => {
    try {
        const res = await axios.get(
            'https://api.github.com/search/users?q=greg'
        );
        console.log(res.data.items);
    } catch (e) {
    }
});
```

Actions after the *await* keyword are not executed until the promise resolves, meaning the code will wait. When we use *await*, we have to add *async* to the function declaring that it is making the request as an asynchronous function.

After *await*, we have *console.log(res.data.items)*. Note that we access *data.items* property to get the *items* array direct as that is the JSON structure of the GitHub response. So when our AJAX call is completed, we print the list of items returned which is the GitHub users search results.

onMount

Now, we come to an important question. What's *onMount*? And why do we place our data request and retrieval code in it?

Every Svelte component fires several lifecycle events we can hook on:
- *onMount* is fired after the component is rendered
- *onDestroy* is fired after the component is rendered
- *beforeUpdate* is fired before the component is updated
- *afterUpdated* is fired after the component is updated

After our GitHub component first renders, we want to make the API data request. Thus, we place our data retrieval code in *onMount*.
Note that we need to import *onMount* from the *svelte* package.

Running our App

Before we run our app, remember that we have to import and call our GitHub component in App.svelte:

Replace Entire Code

```
<script>
    import GitHub from './components/GitHub.svelte';
</script>

<main>
    <GitHub />
</main>
```

Now run your app in Chrome. Go to 'View', 'Developer', 'Developer Tools'. Under console, you can see the following result from the console (fig. 2).

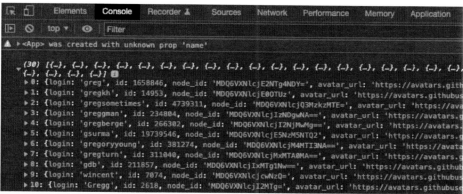

Figure 2

Our requested JSON object is a single object containing an items array of size 30 with each item representing the data of a GitHub user.

Each *user* object has properties *avatar_url*, *html_url*, *login*, *score*, and so on (fig. 3).

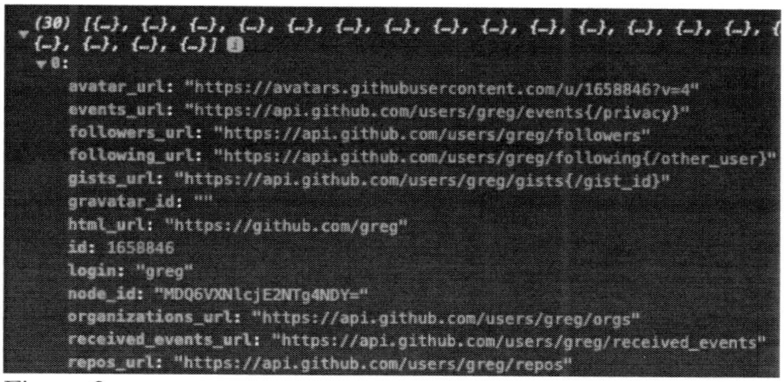

Figure 3

Storing Results in State

Now that we have made a successful connection to our API, let's have a state variable to store our results instead of just logging them to the console. This will let us be able to display the results to the user. Add in the following code in **bold**:

Modify Bold Code

```
<script>
import { onMount } from 'svelte';
import axios from 'axios';

let users = [];

onMount(async () => {
    try {
        const res = await axios.get(
            'https://api.github.com/search/users?q=greg'
        );
        users = res.data.items;
    } catch (e) {
    }
});
</script>
```

We declare the state variable *users* and set it to an initial value of an empty array, [ ]. A variable in state can be set to any type, String, Array, Boolean, Integer, Object etc.

And after *await*, instead of logging to the console, we assign the results to *users*.

Implementing a GitHub Results Display Page

We will now implement a page which displays our GitHub user data nicely like in figure 4.

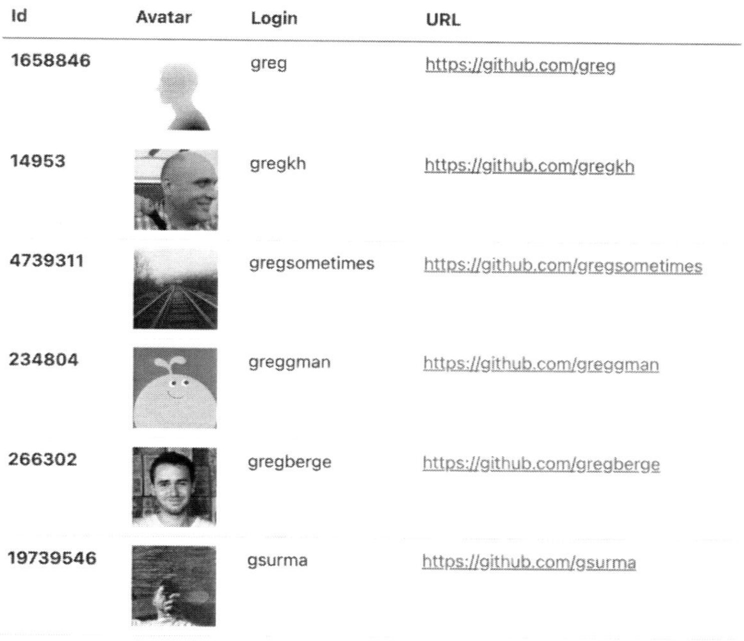

Id	Avatar	Login	URL
1658846		greg	https://github.com/greg
14953		gregkh	https://github.com/gregkh
4739311		gregsometimes	https://github.com/gregsometimes
234804		greggman	https://github.com/greggman
266302		gregberge	https://github.com/gregberge
19739546		gsurma	https://github.com/gsurma

Figure 4

We want to render our GitHub user data nicely. In our markup, we will use the Table component in SvelteStrap (https://sveltestrap.js.org/?path=/story/components--table).

We will slightly modify the markup and include it in our component as shown below:

Modify Bold Code
```
<script>
import { onMount } from 'svelte';
import axios from 'axios';
import { Table } from 'sveltestrap';

let users = [];

onMount(async () => {
    try {
        const res = await axios.get(
            'https://api.github.com/search/users?q=greg'
        );
        users = res.data.items;
    } catch (e) {
    }
});
```

```
</script>

<Table>
    <thead>
      <tr>
        <th>Id</th>
        <th>Avatar</th>
        <th>Login</th>
        <th>URL</th>
      </tr>
    </thead>
    <tbody>
    {#each users as user}
      <tr>
        <th scope="row">{user.id}</th>
        <td><img alt={user.login} src="{user.avatar_url}" width="75"
height="75"/></td>
        <td>{user.login}</td>
        <td><a href="{user.html_url}">{user.html_url}</a></td>
      </tr>
    {/each}
    </tbody>
</Table>
```

Code Explanation

We use the *each* loop to repeat the table row for each user data we get from GitHub.

We then add Javascript expressions wrapped in {} inside the template. The user's id, login, html_url, and avatar_url.

Analyze Code

```
    {#each users as user}
      <tr>
        <th scope="row">{user.id}</th>
        <td><img alt={user.login} src="{user.avatar_url}" width="75"
height="75"/></td>
        <td>{user.login}</td>
        <td><a href="{user.html_url}">{user.html_url}</a></td>
      </tr>
    {/each}
```

We resize the user picture i.e.: *user.avatar_url* with *width*, *height* attributes. We also create a href link with *user.html_url*. When you click it, you are brought to the user's GitHub page.

If you run your app now, you should get a similar page as shown below (fig. 5).

70

Id	Avatar	Login	URL
1658846		greg	https://github.com/greg
14953		gregkh	https://github.com/gregkh
4739311		gregsometimes	https://github.com/gregsometimes
234804		greggman	https://github.com/greggman
266302		gregberge	https://github.com/gregberge
19739546		gsurma	https://github.com/gsurma

Figure 5

Adding an Input to GitHub Results Display Page

We are currently hard-coding our search term to 'greg' in our request to GitHub. Let's create a state variable searchTerm so that a user can type in her search terms and retrieve the relevant search results.

Declare and append searchTerm to our url by adding the below codes in **bold**:

```
                    Modify Bold Code
<script>
import { onMount } from 'svelte';
import axios from 'axios';
import { Table } from 'sveltestrap';

let users = [];
let searchTerm = '';

onMount(async () => {
    try {
        const res = await axios.get(
            `https://api.github.com/search/users?q=${searchTerm}`
        );
```

```
        users = res.data.items;
    } catch (e) {
    }
});
</script>
```

...

Take note that we change from using double quotes `""` to using backticks `` ` `` to allow appending the search term in the above manner.

Next, we encapsulate the above code into a separate function *getData()* so that it can be called both by *onMount* and when a user clicks 'Submit' on a search form. Make the following code changes:

Modify Bold Code

...

```
const getData = async () => {
    try {
        const res = await axios.get(
            `https://api.github.com/search/users?q=${searchTerm}`
        );
        users = res.data.items;
    } catch (e) {
    }
};

onMount(getData());

const handleSubmit = event => {
    event.preventDefault();
    getData();
};
</script>
```

...

Next, add the *<Form>* SvelteStrap component as shown in **bold**:

Modify Bold Code

```
<script>
import { onMount } from 'svelte';
import axios from 'axios';
import { Table, Button, Form, FormGroup, Input } from 'sveltestrap';

...
</script>
```

```
<Form on:submit={handleSubmit}>
    <FormGroup floating label="Search">
        <Input type="text" bind:value={searchTerm} />
    </FormGroup>
    <Button type="submit" color="primary">Submit</Button>
</Form>

<Table>
    …
```

When you run your app now, it render a simple form with a single input (fig. 6) binded to the state's *searchTerm* property.

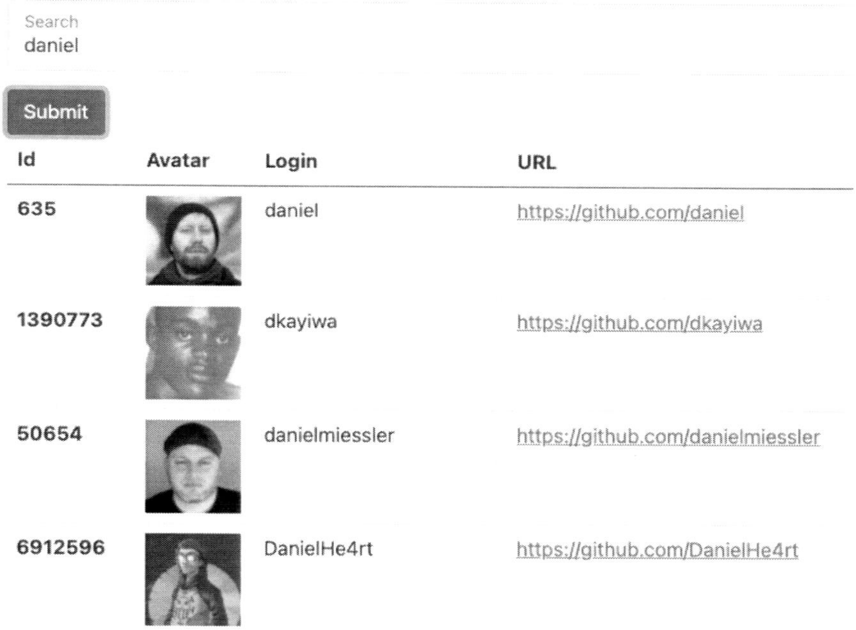
Search
daniel
Submit
Id
Avatar
Login
URL
635
daniel
https://github.com/daniel
1390773
dkayiwa
https://github.com/dkayiwa
50654
danielmiessler
https://github.com/danielmiessler
6912596
DanielHe4rt
https://github.com/DanielHe4rt

Figure 6

When the user types in a search term and clicks 'Search', you can now see GitHub user results.

Showing a Loader Icon

While getting content from a server, it is often useful to show a loading icon to the user (fig. 7).

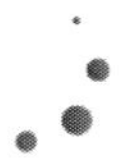

figure 7

To do so, in GitHub component, create a state variable called *isLoading* and set it to *true* like in the below code.

Modify Bold Code

```
<script>
import { onMount } from 'svelte';
import axios from 'axios';
import { Table, Button, Form, FormGroup, Input } from 'sveltestrap';

let users = [];
let searchTerm = '';
let isLoading = false;

...
```

isLoading will be true when loading of results from the server is still going on. We set it to false in the beginning.

We set *isLoading* to true before the call to *axios.get* in *handleSubmit* (called when a user submits the form):

Modify Bold Code

```
...

const handleSubmit = event => {
    event.preventDefault();
    isLoading = true;
    getData();
};
</script>

...
```

Once we are notified of results from the GitHub request, we set *isLoading* to *false* in *getData* to hide the spinner:

Modify Bold Code

```
...

const getData = async () => {
    try {
        const res = await axios.get(
```

```
            `https://api.github.com/search/users?q=${searchTerm}`
        );
        users = res.data.items;
        isLoading = false;
    } catch (e) {
    }
};
```

...

Next in the markup, we render a spinner:

Modify Bold Code

```
<script>
import { onMount } from 'svelte';
import axios from 'axios';
import { Table, Button, Form, FormGroup, Input, Spinner } from
'sveltestrap';

...

</script>

<Form on:submit={handleSubmit}>
    ...
</Form>

{#if isLoading}
    <Spinner color='primary' />
{/if}

<Table>
    ...
```

We use the *if* conditional to make the *Spinner* visible only when the component is loading. SvelteStrap provides many easy to use spinners (sveltestrap.js.org/?path=/story/components--spinner fig. 8).

Spinner

Bootstrap Spinner

Colors

EXAMPLE

Figure 8

Running your App

If you load your app in the browser, you should see the Spinner being displayed for a short moment before data from the server is loaded.

You can try out other kinds of animations as specified in the SvelteStrap documentation.

Summary

In the chapter, we learned how to implement a GitHub User Search application by connecting our React app to the GitHub RESTful API using Axios, Promises, component lifecycles and displaying a loader icon.

Contact support@i-ducate.com if you have not already had the full source code for this chapter.

CHAPTER 8: TODO C.R.U.D. APP

Project Setup for our ToDo C.R.U.D. App

In this chapter, we will create a ToDo app to create, read, update, delete and mark-complete todos (fig. 1).

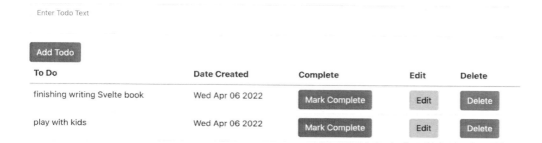

Figure 1

In the next chapter, we will then see how to connect our app to an external API to persist our data. This app will teach you fundamentals on how to build larger and more complicated apps, in particular using the Svelte store.

First, create a new project with:

Execute in Terminal

```
npm init vite sveltetodo
```

Then, you will be asked some questions. Follow the next instructions:
- "Need to install the following packages: create-vite". Type 'y', and press 'Enter'. This will only appear if you had not installed this package before.
- "Select a framework". Select 'svelte', and press 'Enter'.
- "Select a variant". Select 'svelte', and press 'Enter'.

Next, run the following:

Execute in Terminal

```
cd sveltetodo
npm install
```

Next, we install the *axios* and *uuid* library with:

Execute in Terminal

```
npm install axios uuid
```

We are familiar with *axios* as we have used it before. *uuid* is used to create unique id values for each of our todos.

Next, install SvelteStrap with:

Execute in Terminal

```
npm install sveltestrap svelte
```

Include the link to use SvelteStrap in *index.html*:

Modify Bold Code

```
<!DOCTYPE html>
<html lang="en">
  <head>
    <meta charset="UTF-8" />
    <link rel="icon" href="/favicon.ico" />
    <meta name="viewport" content="width=device-width, initial-scale=1.0"
/>
    <title>Svelte + Vite App</title>
    <link rel="stylesheet"
href="https://cdn.jsdelivr.net/npm/bootstrap@5.1.0/dist/css/bootstrap.min
.css">
  </head>
  <body>
    <div id="app"></div>
    <script type="module" src="/src/main.js"></script>
  </body>
</html>
```

Stores

We will use a store to define our initial *todos*. Now what are stores and why do we use them?

You can imagine that we will need to pass around our todos via props quite a lot for example:
- after adding a todo, pass it back to the ToDo List,
- when user selects a todo to edit, pass it to the edit form and then pass it back to the ToDo List

To help us manage our app's state of todos, we will use stores so that our components (i.e. ToDoList, ToDoForm, ToDoEditForm - implemented later) can talk to each other without passing props around too much.

So, in a new file /src/stores.js, define our initial *todos* with the following code:

Add Code

```
import {writable} from 'svelte/store';

export const TodoStore = writable([
  {
      id:1,
      text: "finishing writing Svelte book",
      complete: false,
      date: new Date().toDateString(),
      dateCompleted: null
  },
    {
      id:2,
      text: "play with kids",
      complete: false,
      date: new Date().toDateString(),
      dateCompleted: null
  },
    {
      id:3,
      text: "read bible",
      complete: false,
      date: new Date().toDateString(),
      dateCompleted: null
  }
]);
```

Code Explanation

Analyze Code

```
import {writable} from 'svelte/store';

export const TodoStore = writable([…]);
```

We first import writable from 'svelte/store' and create a store variable *TodoStore* using the writable function. We pass an array of *todo* objects as the default *todos* state.

79

We put the store in a separate file store.js, so that it can be imported into multiple components. And since store is not a component, it can be a *.js* file instead of *.svelte* file.

ToDoList component

In *src*, create a new folder *components*. In it, create a new file *ToDoList.svelte* to list our todos with the following code:

Add Code

```
<script>
import {TodoStore} from '../stores';
</script>

{#each $TodoStore as todo (todo.id)}
    <li>{todo.text}</li>
{/each}
```

Code Explanation

We first import TodoStore we implemented earlier to access the todos store. We then proceed to *loop* and list out the todo items contained in TodoStore.

Running our App

Back in *App.js*, import *ToDoList* and render it:

Replace Entire Code

```
<script>
    import ToDoList from './components/ToDoList.svelte';
</script>

<main>
        <ToDoList />
</main>
```

If you run your app now, you should see an initial list of *todos* displayed (fig. 2).

- finishing writing Svelte book
- play with kids
- read bible

Figure 2

Styling our *ToDoList*

Our list of todos looks rather plain. Let's apply some styling from SvelteStrap. We will use the *Table* component (https://sveltestrap.js.org/?path=/story/components--table) to list our todos in a table.

In *src/components/ToDoList.js*, add the following:

```
                            Modify Bold Code
<script>
import {TodoStore} from '../stores';
import { Table } from 'sveltestrap';
</script>

<Table>
    <thead>
      <tr>
        <th>To Do</th>
        <th>Date Created</th>
        <th>Complete</th>
        <th>Edit</th>
        <th>Delete</th>
      </tr>
    </thead>
    <tbody>
      {#each $TodoStore as todo (todo.id)}
        <tr>
          <td>{todo.text}</td>
          <td>{todo.date}</td>
          <td>Mark Complete</td>
          <td>Edit</td>
          <td>Delete</td>
        </tr>
      {/each}
    </tbody>
</Table>
```

Our table has five columns, the Todo text, date created, Mark-Complete, *Edit* and *Delete* columns.

And when we run our app now, our *todos* should be nicely displayed (fig. 3):

To Do	Date Created	Complete	Edit	Delete
finishing writing Svelte book	Wed Apr 06 2022	Mark Complete	Edit	Delete
play with kids	Wed Apr 06 2022	Mark Complete	Edit	Delete
read bible	Wed Apr 06 2022	Mark Complete	Edit	Delete

Figure 3

Removing a Todo

Now, let's see how we remove (delete) a todo. We want to remove a todo upon clicking on 'Delete'. In the delete *td*, add a Button with its *on:click* handler:

Modify Bold Code

```
<script>
import {TodoStore} from '../stores';
import { Table, Button } from 'sveltestrap';
</script>

<Table>
    <thead>
      ...
    </thead>
    <tbody>
      {#each $TodoStore as todo (todo.id)}
        <tr>
          <td>{todo.text}</td>
          <td>{todo.date}</td>
          <td>Mark Complete</td>
          <td>Edit</td>
          <td>
            <Button on:click={() => handleDelete(todo.id)}
color='danger'>
                Delete
            </Button>
          </td>
        </tr>
      {/each}
    </tbody>
</Table>
```

The *on:click* fires *handleDelete()*. We provide the todo.id to *handleDelete*. And because 'delete' is a dangerous action, we set its color to 'danger'.

We next implement *handleDelete* by adding in <script>:

```
                          Modify Bold Code
<script>
import {TodoStore} from '../stores';
import { Table, Button } from 'sveltestrap';

const handleDelete = (todoId) => {
    TodoStore.update(currentTodos => {
        return currentTodos.filter(todo => todo.id != todoId)
    });
};
</script>
...
```

Using Stores, we can directly access the todos array directly. We update the store using the *update()* function. We pass in a callback function that is passed the current value as its argument.

We can then add logic in the callback function. For example, *currentTodos.filter* checks for each element and filters for only *todos* whose id is not equal to the id of the todo to be deleted.

If we run our app now, and click on 'Delete' for a todo, that todo will be removed (fig. 4).

To Do	Date Created	Complete	Edit	Delete
finishing writing Svelte book	Wed Apr 06 2022	Mark Complete	Edit	Delete
play with kids	Wed Apr 06 2022	Mark Complete	Edit	Delete

Figure 4

Adding Todos

To let users create a todo, we will have a form on the top of our *ToDoList* component (fig. 5).

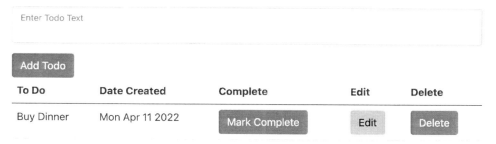

To Do	Date Created	Complete	Edit	Delete
Buy Dinner	Mon Apr 11 2022	Mark Complete	Edit	Delete

Figure 5

We went through forms in chapter six. So we will skip some explanations regarding implementation of a form. In /src/components, create a file ToDoForm.svelte.

Add in the below codes into ToDoForm.svelte:

Add Code

```
<script>
import {v4 as uuidv4} from 'uuid';
import { TodoStore } from '../stores';
import {Form, FormGroup, Input, Alert, Button} from 'sveltestrap';

let text = '';
let textErrorMessage = '';

const handleSubmit = event => {
    event.preventDefault();
};
</script>

<Form on:submit={handleSubmit}>
    <FormGroup floating label="Enter Todo Text">
        <Input type="text" bind:value={text} />
    </FormGroup>
    {#if textErrorMessage.length > 0}
        <Alert color="danger">
            {textErrorMessage}
        </Alert>
    {/if}
    <Button type="submit" color="primary">Add Todo</Button>
</Form>
```

Code Explanation

Analyze Code

```
import {v4 as uuidv4} from 'uuid';
import { TodoStore } from '../stores';
import {Form, FormGroup, Input, Alert, Button} from 'sveltestrap';
```

We import uuidv4 to provide unique identifiers for our todos.
We import the *Form*, FormGroup, Input, Alert and *Button* component from SvelteStrap to use in our form.

Analyze Code

```
let text = '';
let textErrorMessage = '';
```

We store the user-entered todo text in *text*. We store any error messages related to *text* in *textErrorMessage*.

We declare a *handleSubmit* (we will add in more details later) and bind it to the Form's *submit* event.

Analyze Code

```
const handleSubmit = event => {
    event.preventDefault();
};
</script>

<Form on:submit={handleSubmit}>
...
```

In our form, we have a form input control for users to enter the todo text. We bind the input control's *value* to *text*. We also show *textErrorMessage* (if any) in a danger Alert.

These steps should be familiar to you as we have gone through them in chapter six.

Analyze Code

```
<Form on:submit={handleSubmit}>
    <FormGroup floating label="Enter Todo Text">
        <Input type="text" bind:value={text} />
    </FormGroup>
    {#if textErrorMessage.length > 0}
        <Alert color="danger">
            {textErrorMessage}
        </Alert>
    {/if}
    <Button type="submit" color="primary">Add Todo</Button>
</Form>
```

handleSubmit

We then implement *handleSubmit* with:

Modify Bold Code

```
<script>
…

let text = '';
let textErrorMessage = '';
let validText = false;

const handleSubmit = event => {
    event.preventDefault();
    handleInput();
    if(validText){
        const newTodo = {
            id: uuidv4(),
            text: text,
            complete:false,
            date: new Date().toDateString(),
            dateCompleted: false
        };

        TodoStore.update(currentTodos =>{
            return [newTodo, ...currentTodos]
        });
        // to clear field after adding

        text = "";
        validText = false;
    }
};

const handleInput = () => {
    validText = false;
    if(text.length < 10){
        textErrorMessage = "Todo text should be minimum 10 characters";
    }
    else{
        textErrorMessage = '';
        validText = true;
    }
};
</script>
```

Code Explantion

The *handleInput* function's validation should be familiar to you as they are what we have gone through in chapter six for validating inputs.

Analyze Code

```
...
if(validText){
    const newTodo = {
        id: uuidv4(),
        text: text,
        complete:false,
        date: new Date().toDateString(),
        dateCompleted: false
    };
    ...
```

In *handleSubmit*, we first check if *validText* returns true. If so, we create a new todo object. Using the imported uuid library, we use uuidv4() to generate a unique id. We also assign text with the user-input text.
We set the todo creation date to the current date with *new Date()*.

Analyze Code

```
TodoStore.update(currentTodos =>{
    return [newTodo, ...currentTodos]
});
```

We create a new array with the existing *currentTodos* ('...' spread operator) and adding *newToDo* to it.

Running our App

Before we run our app, we need to import and render the ToDoForm component in App.svelte:

Modify Bold Code

```
<script>
    import ToDoList from './components/ToDoList.svelte';
    import ToDoForm from './components/ToDoForm.svelte';
</script>

<main>
    <ToDoForm />
    <ToDoList />
</main>
```

And when we run our app, our TodoForm will appear. If we enter a todo with less than 10 characters, we will get an alert (fig. 6).

87

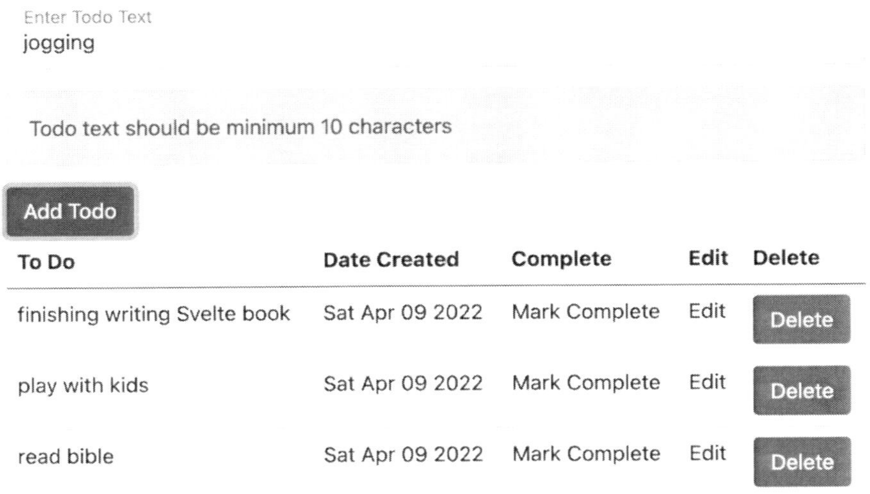

Enter Todo Text

jogging

Todo text should be minimum 10 characters

To Do	Date Created	Complete	Edit	Delete
finishing writing Svelte book	Sat Apr 09 2022	Mark Complete	Edit	Delete
play with kids	Sat Apr 09 2022	Mark Complete	Edit	Delete
read bible	Sat Apr 09 2022	Mark Complete	Edit	Delete

Figure 6

If we enter a valid todo text, it gets added to the todo list (fig. 7).

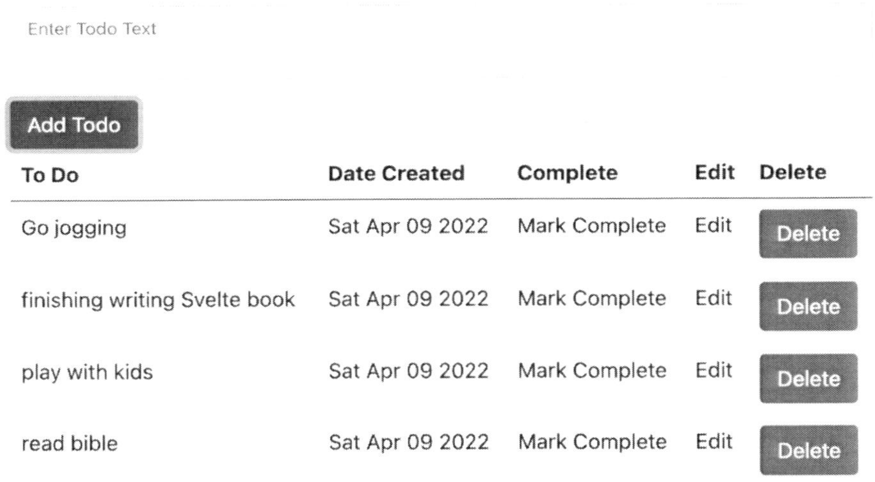

Enter Todo Text

Add Todo

To Do	Date Created	Complete	Edit	Delete
Go jogging	Sat Apr 09 2022	Mark Complete	Edit	Delete
finishing writing Svelte book	Sat Apr 09 2022	Mark Complete	Edit	Delete
play with kids	Sat Apr 09 2022	Mark Complete	Edit	Delete
read bible	Sat Apr 09 2022	Mark Complete	Edit	Delete

Figure 7

Editing Todos

Next, we want to implement editing our todos. A user will first click on the 'Edit' of the todo she wishes to edit, and that todo text will appear in the form field for her to edit.

App.svelte

To do so, we add an *editMode* and *editTodo* to *App.svelte*'s local state.

Modify Bold Code

```
<script>
      import ToDoList from './components/ToDoList.svelte';
      import ToDoForm from './components/ToDoForm.svelte';

      let editMode = false;
      let editTodo = null;
</script>
```

...

editMode will be set to true when a user clicks on a 'Edit'. *editTodo* will contain the specific todo object to be edited.

We render a separate ToDoEditForm (similar to ToDoForm) that when *editMode* is true, will be rendered instead of ToDoForm. We pass in *editTodo* into ToDoForm as props.

Modify Bold Code

...

```
<main>
      {#if editMode}
            <ToDoEditForm editTodo={editTodo} />
      {:else}
            <ToDoForm />
      {/if}
      <ToDoList />
</main>
```

ToDoList.svelte

But where do we get *editTodo* from? We will need to get it from ToDoList. Add an Edit button in each row of ToDoList with the below code:

Modify Bold Code

```
     ...
      {#each $TodoStore as todo (todo.id)}
        <tr>
          <td>{todo.text}</td>
          <td>{todo.date}</td>
          <td>Mark Complete</td>
          <td>
```

89

```
        <Button on:click={() => handleEdit(todo)} color='warning'>
            Edit
        </Button>
      </td>
      <td>
        <Button on:click={() => handleDelete(todo.id)}
color='danger'>
            Delete
        </Button>
      </td>
    </tr>
  {/each}
  ...
```

The button calls *handleEdit* which takes in the todo to be edited. Implement *handleEdit* by adding the below codes in **bold**:

Modify Bold Code

```
<script>
import {TodoStore} from '../stores';
import { Table, Button } from 'sveltestrap';
import {createEventDispatcher} from 'svelte';

const dispatch = createEventDispatcher();

const handleEdit = (todo) => {
    dispatch('edit-todo', todo)
};

...
```

Because we need to pass the todo to be edited back to App.svelte, in *handleEdit* we dispatch our own custom event 'edit-todo'. We need to import *createEventDispatcher* from the 'svelte' package and call it to get an event dispatcher.
We then dispatch 'edit-todo' with `dispatch('edit-todo', todo)`.

The first argument 'edit-todo' is our custom event name and the second argument is the data we want to pass in. In doing so, we can then pass the todo to be edited to App.svelte.

App.svelte

We need to register the 'edit-todo' event with ToDoList. Thus, back in App.svelte, add:

Modify Bold Code

...

```
<main>
      {#if editMode}
            <ToDoEditForm editTodo={editTodo} />
      {:else}
            <ToDoForm />
      {/if}
      <ToDoList on:edit-todo={editTodoEvent} />
</main>
```

Thus, we are saying that ToDoList will trigger a custom event 'edit-todo' and call the function *editTodoEvent*. We then define editTodoEvent as:

Modify Bold Code

```
<script>
      import ToDoList from './components/ToDoList.svelte';
      import ToDoForm from './components/ToDoForm.svelte';

      let editMode = false;
      let editTodo = null;

      const editTodoEvent = (event) => {
            editMode = true;
            editTodo = event.detail;
      };
</script>
```

...

editTodoEvent will set *editMode* to true and provide us with the todo to be edited (available on the *event* object – passed in via the second parameter to *dispatch()*).

We can then pass *editTodo* into ToDoEditForm:

Analyze Code

```
      {#if editMode}
            <ToDoEditForm editTodo={editTodo} />
      {:else}
```

We then need to import the ToDoEditForm (which will be created next). Make the following changes in **bold** in App.svelte:

91

Modify Bold Code

```
<script>
    import ToDoList from './components/ToDoList.svelte';
    import ToDoForm from './components/ToDoForm.svelte';
    import ToDoEditForm from './components/ToDoEditForm.svelte';
    ...
```

ToDoEditForm

ToDoEditForm will be quite similar to ToDoForm. We can in fact combine them, but for simplicity's sake in learning, we create a separate form.

In *components*, create a new file ToDoEditForm.svelte and copy paste the codes from ToDoForm.svelte into it.

Make the following changes:

Modify Bold Code

```
<script>
import {v4 as uuidv4} from 'uuid';
import { TodoStore } from '../stores';
import {Form, FormGroup, Input, Alert, Button} from 'sveltestrap';

export let editTodo = null;
let text = '';
let textErrorMessage = '';
let validText = false;


...
```

We create the *editTodo* prop to receive it from App.svelte. We will use editTodo to populate our Edit Form. And because of this, we make a slight change to *handleInput*:

Modify Bold Code

```
...

const handleInput = () => {
    validText = false;
    if(editTodo.text.length < 10){
        textErrorMessage = "Todo text should be minimum 10 characters";
    }
    else{
        textErrorMessage = '';
        validText = true;
    }
};
```

```
</script>
...
```

And also to the Form:

Modify Bold Code

```
...
```

```
<Form on:submit={handleSubmit}>
    <FormGroup floating label="Enter Todo Text">
        <Input type="text" bind:value={editTodo.text} />
    </FormGroup>
    {#if textErrorMessage.length > 0}
        <Alert color="danger">
            {textErrorMessage}
        </Alert>
    {/if}
    <Button type="submit" color="primary">Edit Todo</Button>
</Form>
```

With this, we populate the form's field with the todo's text to be edited.

Testing our App

Now let's test our app to see if we can populate the Edit form when we click on a particular todo.

And when you run your app and click on a todo, the text appears in the form's field for you to edit (fig. 8). Notice: you could need to stop and run the server again.

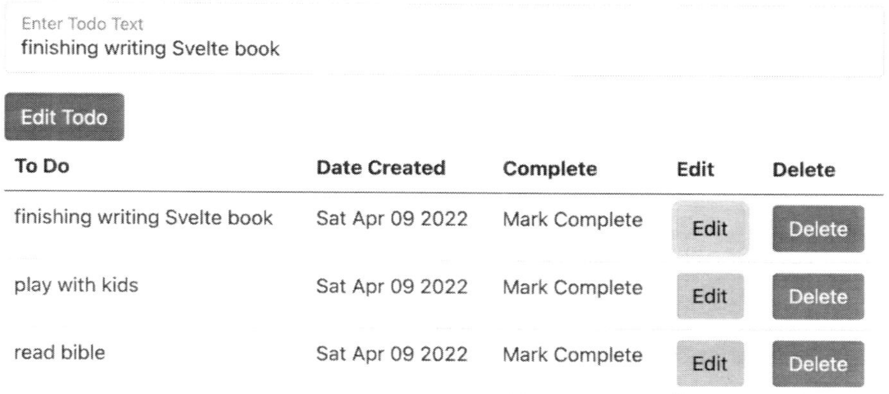

To Do	Date Created	Complete	Edit	Delete
finishing writing Svelte book	Sat Apr 09 2022	Mark Complete	Edit	Delete
play with kids	Sat Apr 09 2022	Mark Complete	Edit	Delete
read bible	Sat Apr 09 2022	Mark Complete	Edit	Delete

Figure 8

Notice that the button's text also changes to 'Edit Todo' since we are displaying ToDoEditForm instead of ToDoForm now.

handleSubmit

Now that we have populated the Edit Form, let's implement the actual editing of the todo.

In *ToDoEditForm.svelte*, in *handleSubmit*, we make the following changes.

Modify Bold Code

...

```
const handleSubmit = event => {
    event.preventDefault();
    handleInput();
    if(validText){
        const editedTodo = {
            ...editTodo,
            text: editTodo.text
        };

        TodoStore.update(currentTodos => {
            const updatedToDoIndex = currentTodos.findIndex(
                t => t.id === editedTodo.id
            );
            const updatedToDos = [
                ...currentTodos.slice(0,updatedToDoIndex),
                editedTodo,
                ...currentTodos.slice(updatedToDoIndex + 1)
            ];
            return updatedToDos;
        });
    }
};
```

...

Code Explanation

Analyze Code

```
const editedTodo = {
    ...editTodo,
    text: editTodo.text
};
```

94

First, we have editedToDo which keeps the existing todo values and updates the todo text.

Now, because there is no straightforward function to find an element and then change its content, we have to actually 'slice' up our array to get the items before and after the selected element, and in between, insert *editedToDo*.

We first get the index of the selected element with:

Analyze Code
```
const updatedToDoIndex = currentTodos.findIndex(
    t => t.id === editedTodo.id
);
```

And to get the items before the selected element, we use
`currentTodos.slice(0,updatedToDoIndex)`

To get the items after the selected element, we use:
`currentTodos.slice(updatedToDoIndex + 1)`

And to create a new array with the changed todo in between, we have:

Analyze Code
```
const updatedToDos = [
    ...currentTodos.slice(0,updatedToDoIndex),
    editedTodo,
    ...currentTodos.slice(updatedToDoIndex + 1)
];
```

Running our App

When we run our app now, we can select a todo and then update its text.

Problem

There is still a problem though. After editing a todo, the Form that displays in our app is the ToDoEditForm. We ought to default this back to the ToDoForm for adding todos.

To do so, we will dispatch a custom event to App.svelte to announce that the editing has finished.

Add the below lines into src/components/ToDoEditForm.svelte:

Modify Bold Code

```
<script>
import { TodoStore } from '../stores';
import {Form, FormGroup, Input, Alert, Button} from 'sveltestrap';
import { createEventDispatcher } from "svelte";

export let editTodo = null;
let textErrorMessage = '';
let validText = false;

const dispatch = createEventDispatcher();

const handleSubmit = event => {
    event.preventDefault();
    handleInput();
    if(validText){

        …

        TodoStore.update(currentTodos => {

            …

        });

        dispatch('finish-edit');
    }
};

…
```

Back in src/App.svelte, add:

Modify Bold Code

```
<script>

    …

    const finishEdit = (event) => {
        editMode = false;
    };
</script>

<main>
    {#if editMode}
        <ToDoEditForm editTodo={editTodo} on:finish-edit={finishEdit} />
    {:else}
        <ToDoForm />
    {/if}
    <ToDoList on:edit-todo={editTodoEvent} />
</main>
```

That is, when ToDoEditForm generates the *finish-edit* event, set *editMode* back to false in App.svelte.

And when you run your app now, and after editing a todo, it will default back to the ToDoForm to allow adding of todos.

Summary

Congratulations if you made it thus far! In the next chapter, we will see how to persist our data by connecting to an external API.

And in case you are lost, below's the full source code.

App.svelte

Analyze Code

```
<script>
    import ToDoList from './components/ToDoList.svelte';
    import ToDoForm from './components/ToDoForm.svelte';
    import ToDoEditForm from './components/ToDoEditForm.svelte';

    let editMode = false;
    let editTodo = null;

    const editTodoEvent = (event) => {
        editMode = true;
        editTodo = event.detail;
    };

    const finishEdit = (event) => {
        editMode = false;
    };
</script>

<main>
    {#if editMode}
        <ToDoEditForm editTodo={editTodo} on:finish-edit={finishEdit}
/>
    {:else}
        <ToDoForm />
    {/if}
    <ToDoList on:edit-todo={editTodoEvent} />
</main>
```

ToDoList.svelte

Analyze Code

```
<script>
import {TodoStore} from '../stores';
import { Table, Button } from 'sveltestrap';
import {createEventDispatcher} from 'svelte';

const dispatch = createEventDispatcher();

const handleEdit = (todo) => {
    dispatch('edit-todo', todo)
};

const handleDelete = (todoId) => {
    TodoStore.update(currentTodos => {
            return currentTodos.filter(todo => todo.id != todoId)
    });
};
</script>

<Table>
    <thead>
      <tr>
        <th>To Do</th>
        <th>Date Created</th>
        <th>Complete</th>
        <th>Edit</th>
        <th>Delete</th>
      </tr>
    </thead>
    <tbody>
      {#each $TodoStore as todo (todo.id)}
        <tr>
          <td>{todo.text}</td>
          <td>{todo.date}</td>
          <td>Mark Complete</td>
          <td>
            <Button on:click={() => handleEdit(todo)} color='warning'>
                Edit
            </Button>
          </td>
          <td>
            <Button on:click={() => handleDelete(todo.id)}
color='danger'>
                Delete
            </Button>
          </td>
```

```
        </tr>
      {/each}
    </tbody>
</Table>
```

ToDoForm.svelte

Analyze Code

```
<script>
import {v4 as uuidv4} from 'uuid';
import { TodoStore } from '../stores';
import {Form, FormGroup, Input, Alert, Button} from 'sveltestrap';

let text = '';
let textErrorMessage = '';
let validText = false;

const handleSubmit = event => {
    event.preventDefault();
    handleInput();
    if(validText){
        const newTodo = {
            id: uuidv4(),
            text: text,
            complete:false,
            date: new Date().toDateString(),
            dateCompleted: false
        };

        TodoStore.update(currentTodos =>{
            return [newTodo, ...currentTodos]
        });
        // to clear field after adding

        text = "";
        validText = false;
    }
};

const handleInput = () => {
    validText = false;
    if(text.length < 10){
        textErrorMessage = "Todo text should be minimum 10 characters";
    }
    else{
        textErrorMessage = '';
        validText = true;
    }
```

```
};
</script>

<Form on:submit={handleSubmit}>
    <FormGroup floating label="Enter Todo Text">
        <Input type="text" bind:value={text} />
    </FormGroup>
    {#if textErrorMessage.length > 0}
        <Alert color="danger">
            {textErrorMessage}
        </Alert>
    {/if}
    <Button type="submit" color="primary">Add Todo</Button>
</Form>
```

ToDoEditForm.svelte

Analyze Code

```
<script>
import { TodoStore } from '../stores';
import {Form, FormGroup, Input, Alert, Button} from 'sveltestrap';
import { createEventDispatcher } from "svelte";

export let editTodo = null;
let textErrorMessage = '';
let validText = false;

const dispatch = createEventDispatcher();

const handleSubmit = event => {
    event.preventDefault();
    handleInput();
    if(validText){
        const editedTodo = {
            ...editTodo,
            text: editTodo.text
        };

        TodoStore.update(currentTodos => {
            const updatedToDoIndex = currentTodos.findIndex(
                t => t.id === editedTodo.id
            );
            const updatedToDos = [
                ...currentTodos.slice(0,updatedToDoIndex),
                editedTodo,
                ...currentTodos.slice(updatedToDoIndex + 1)
            ];
            return updatedToDos;
```

100

```
        });

        dispatch('finish-edit');
    }
};

const handleInput = () => {
    validText = false;
    if(editTodo.text.length < 10){
        textErrorMessage = "Todo text should be minimum 10 characters";
    }
    else{
        textErrorMessage = '';
        validText = true;
    }
};
</script>

<Form on:submit={handleSubmit}>
    <FormGroup floating label="Enter Todo Text">
        <Input type="text" bind:value={editTodo.text} />
    </FormGroup>
    {#if textErrorMessage.length > 0}
        <Alert color="danger">
            {textErrorMessage}
        </Alert>
    {/if}
    <Button type="submit" color="primary">Edit Todo</Button>
</Form>
```

CHAPTER 9: CONNECTING TO AN API TO PERSIST DATA

We have made progress in our todo app. But our data is not yet persistent. That is, when we reload our application, all the changes we have done to our data is gone. In this chapter, we will connect to an API to enable persistency in create, read, update and delete todos.

The API we are connecting to can be supported by any backend, e.g. Nodejs, Firebase, ASP.Net etc. Setting up a backend is obviously beyond the scope of this book. But to quickly set up a mock API, we will use *json-server* (*github.com/typicode/json-server*) which makes it easy for us to set up JSON APIs for use in demos and proof of concepts.

In a new Terminal, go to the folder containing your Svelte projects and run:

Execute in Terminal

```
npm install -g json-server
```

(Note: you might need *sudo*)

Next, create a new folder called *backendapp* and prepare a *todos.json* file which contains the following:

Add Code

```json
{
  "todos": [
    {
      "id": "1",
      "text": "Fetch Kid from Tuition",
      "complete": false,
      "date": "Mon Apr 11 2022",
      "dateCompleted": false
    },
    {
      "id": "2",
      "text": "Buy Dinner",
      "complete": false,
      "date": "Mon Apr 11 2022",
      "dateCompleted": false
    },
    {
      "id": "3",
      "text": "Post on twitter.com/greglim81",
      "complete": false,
      "date": "Mon Apr 11 2022",
```

```
    "dateCompleted": false
  }
 ]
}
```

These are similar to the *todos* we have in *stores.js*:

Back in Terminal, in the folder that contains *todos.json*, run the command:

Execute in Terminal

```
json-server -p 4000 todos.json
```

This will run a mock REST API server in your local machine and you can see the end point at:

```
http://localhost:4000/todos
```

The endpoint will return an array of *todos* just like in our initial state back in *stores.js*.

Now that we have a mock REST API running, let's connect to it from our Svelte app. You can imagine that the REST API is deployed on a server in a real-world scenario. Simply change the url of the endpoint to point to the server. The rest of the code remains the same.

Using *onMount* to Fetch Initial App Data

Because we are retrieving our todos from the API, our initial *todos* in *src/stores.js* (in the *sveltetodo* project) will just be an empty array.

Replace Entire Code

```
import {writable} from 'svelte/store';

export const TodoStore = writable([]);
```

We will next use *onMount* in ToDoList.svelte to call our API. Add the following code:

src/components/ToDoList.svelte

Modify Bold Code

```
<script>
import {TodoStore} from '../stores';
import { Table, Button } from 'sveltestrap';
import {createEventDispatcher, onMount} from 'svelte';
import axios from 'axios';

const endpoint = "http://localhost:4000/todos/";
```

104

```
onMount(async () => {
  try {
    const res = await axios.get(endpoint);
    TodoStore.update(() => {
      return res.data;
    });
  }
  catch(e){}
});
```

...

We use onMount to retrieve data from the endpoint when the component is mounted.

We use *axios.get* with the endpoint to retrieve data from the API and assign the results to the store. Because we use *await* on *axios.get*, we need to specify *async* at the declaration.

When we run our app now, we retrieve our todos from the API and display them.

Delete Request to Remove Todos

To delete a todo, we need to get the specific url for a todo item. We get that by appending the *todo.id* to the endpoint: *endpoint + todo.id*, e.g. *http://localhost:4000/todos/1*

Thus in *ToDoList*, in *handleDelete*, we specify the todo url, *endpoint + todo.id* to *axios.delete* to remove the todo with the codes in **bold**:

Modify Bold Code

```
<script>
...

const handleDelete = async (todoId) => {
    await axios.delete(endpoint + todoId);

    TodoStore.update(currentTodos => {
        return currentTodos.filter(todo => todo.id != todoId)
    });
};
</script>
```

...

Because we use *await* on *axios.delete*, we need to specify *async* at the declaration of the function.

Run your app now and when you delete a todo, it will be removed.

Performing Post Request to Add Todos

Next, we will perform a post request to add a todo. In *ToDoForm.svelte*, add the following codes in **bold**:

```
                          Modify Bold Code
<script>
import {v4 as uuidv4} from 'uuid';
import { TodoStore } from '../stores';
import {Form, FormGroup, Input, Alert, Button} from 'sveltestrap';
import axios from 'axios';

let text = '';
let textErrorMessage = '';
let validText = false;
const endpoint = "http://localhost:4000/todos/";

const handleSubmit = async event => {
    event.preventDefault();
    handleInput();
    if(validText){
        const newTodo = {
            id: uuidv4(),
            text: text,
            complete:false,
            date: new Date().toDateString(),
            dateCompleted: false
        };

        const response = await axios.post(endpoint,newTodo);

        TodoStore.update(currentTodos =>{
            return [newTodo, ...currentTodos]
        });
        // to clear field after adding

        text = "";
        validText = false;
    }
};

...
```

Code Explanation

axios.post requires two parameters. The first parameter is the URL of the service endpoint. The second parameter is the object which contains the properties we want to send to our server.

We thus call *axios.post* with our endpoint and the new todo object *newToDo*. And because we use *await*, we have to label *handleSubmit* as an asynchronous function with the async keyword.

Run your app and you should be able to add todos.

Performing Patch Request to Update Todos

Finally, let's implement editing a todo. Just add a few lines of code to the ToDoEditForm.svelte file!

Modify Bold Code

```
<script>
import { TodoStore } from '../stores';
import {Form, FormGroup, Input, Alert, Button} from 'sveltestrap';
import { createEventDispatcher } from "svelte";
import axios from 'axios';

export let editTodo = null;
let textErrorMessage = '';
let validText = false;
const endpoint = "http://localhost:4000/todos/";

const dispatch = createEventDispatcher();

const handleSubmit = async event => {
    event.preventDefault();
    handleInput();
    if(validText){
        const editedTodo = {
            ...editTodo,
            text: editTodo.text
        };

        await axios.patch(endpoint+editedTodo.id,
            {text:editedTodo.text});

        TodoStore.update(currentTodos => {
            ...
```

We call *patch* with the specific todo's end point and the attribute to be updated (in our case *text*). The rest of the code remains the same. And when we run our app now, we can edit a todo!
In case you got lost in any of the steps, get the full code by contacting support@i-ducate.com.

Chapter 10: Marking Todos Complete

Let's implement a mark 'Complete' button for each Todo in *src/components/ToDoList.svelte* by adding the below in **bold**:

Modify Bold Code

```
...
<tbody>
    {#each $TodoStore as todo (todo.id)}
      {#if !todo.complete}
        <tr>
          <td>{todo.text}</td>
          <td>{todo.date}</td>
          <td>
            <Button on:click={() => toggleComplete(todo)}
color='success'>
                Mark Complete
            </Button>
          </td>
          <td>
            <Button on:click={() => handleEdit(todo)} color='warning'>
                Edit
            </Button>
          </td>
          <td>
            <Button on:click={() => handleDelete(todo.id)}
color='danger'>
                Delete
            </Button>
          </td>
        </tr>
      {/if}
    {/each}
</tbody>
...
```

Next, add in the codes for *toggleComplete* in <script>:

Modify Bold Code

```
...

const toggleComplete = async (todo) => {
  todo.complete = !todo.complete;
  todo.dateCompleted = new Date().toDateString();

  await axios.patch(endpoint+todo.id,{
```

```
    complete:todo.complete,
    dateCompleted: todo.dateCompleted
  });

  TodoStore.update(currentTodos => {
    const updatedToDoIndex = currentTodos.findIndex(
      t => t.id === todo.id
    );

    const updatedToDos = [
      ...currentTodos.slice(0,updatedToDoIndex),
      todo,
      ...currentTodos.slice(updatedToDoIndex + 1)
    ];

    return updatedToDos;
  });
};
</script>

<Table>
```

Code Explanation

Analyze Code

```
    ...
    <tbody>
      {#each $TodoStore as todo (todo.id)}
        {#if !todo.complete}
          ...
```

Using #if, we list only todos that are uncompleted. We will show the completed todos in another section.

Analyze Code

```
        ...
        <tr>
          <td>{todo.text}</td>
          <td>{todo.date}</td>
          <td>
            <Button on:click={() => toggleComplete(todo)}
color='success'>
              Mark Complete
            </Button>
          </td>
```

In the complete button, we pass the todo into *toggleComplete*.

110

Analyze Code

```
const toggleComplete = async (todo) => {
  todo.complete = !todo.complete;
  todo.dateCompleted = new Date().toDateString();

  await axios.patch(endpoint+todo.id,{
    complete:todo.complete,
    dateCompleted: todo.dateCompleted
  });

  TodoStore.update(currentTodos => {
    ...
  });
};
```

toggleComplete is very similar to updating a todo except that it justs toggles the todo's *complete* property from false to true (to indicate completion) and vice-versa. We also set *dateCompleted* to the current date.

Rendering a Completed Todo

Currently, completed todos are no longer shown in the todo list. We want to render completed todos in a separate section (fig. 1).

Figure 1

This is pretty straightforward as the code will be similar to how we list todos. To do so, add the below markup into *ToDoList.svelte*:

Modify Bold Code

```
...

<Table>
   ...
</Table>

<br>
<h1>Completed Todos</h1>
<Table>
  <thead>
    <tr>
      <th>To Do</th>
      <th>Date Completed</th>
      <th>Complete</th>
      <th>Delete</th>
    </tr>
  </thead>
  <tbody>
    {#each $TodoStore as todo (todo.id)}
      {#if todo.complete}
        <tr>
          <td>{todo.text}</td>
          <td>{todo.dateCompleted}</td>
          <td>
            <Button on:click={() => toggleComplete(todo)}>
              Mark Uncomplete
            </Button>
          </td>
          <td><Button on:click={() => handleDelete(todo.id)}
color='danger'>Delete</Button></td>
        </tr>
      {/if}
    {/each}
  </tbody>
</Table>
```

The added codes are similar to how we list todos, except that we now show todos only if *todo.complete* is true. For completed todos, we no longer show an edit button (completed todos shouldn't be edited). We continue to show the delete button (for users to remove them) and also the 'Mark Uncomplete' button (in case user has to work on the todo again).

CHAPTER 11: FINAL TOUCHES

This will be a short chapter to illustrate other Svelte concepts to put final touches to our application.

Svelte Reactivity

Often, some parts of the component's state need to be computed from other variables and recomputed when they change. For example, we want to display the number of total todos, pending todos, and completed todos (fig. 1).

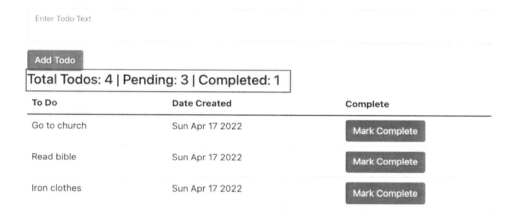

Figure 1

When a user marks a pending todo as complete, the numbers should be recomputed. For these, we use reactive declarations.

In App.svelte, add the following in **bold**:

Modify Bold Code

```
<script>
    import ToDoList from './components/ToDoList.svelte';
    import ToDoForm from './components/ToDoForm.svelte';
    import ToDoEditForm from './components/ToDoEditForm.svelte';
    import { TodoStore } from './stores';

    $: count = $TodoStore.length;
    $: pendingTodosCount = $TodoStore.filter(
            todo => {return !todo.complete}
        ).length;
    $: completedTodosCount = $TodoStore.filter(
            todo => {return todo.complete}
        ).length;

    ...
</script>

<main>
    {#if editMode}
      <ToDoEditForm editTodo={editTodo} on:finish-edit={finishEdit} />
    {:else}
      <ToDoForm />
    {/if}
    <br />
    <h4>Total Todos: {count} | Pending: {pendingTodosCount} |
Completed: {completedTodosCount}</h4>
    <br />
    <ToDoList on:edit-todo={editTodoEvent} />
</main>
```

Code Explanation

With the special syntax *$:*, we listen for changes on *count*, *pendingTodosCount* and *completedTodosCount*. *count* contains the total number of todos in the store.

Analyze Code

```
$: count = $TodoStore.length;
```

pendingTodosCount using the *filter* function, contains only todos that are not completed.

Analyze Code

```
$: pendingTodosCount = $TodoStore.filter(
        todo => {return !todo.complete}
    ).length;
```

114

In a similar fashion, *completedTodosCount* contains only todos that are completed.

Analyze Code
```
$: completedTodosCount = $TodoStore.filter(
        todo => {return todo.complete}
    ).length;
```

When any variable referenced into *count, pendingTodosCount* or *completedTodosCount* changes, Svelte will re-run the computation and update the DOM. That is, as you mark todos 'complete' or 'un-complete', Svelte re-computes the variables and updates the UI.

Transitions

Let's make our user interface more appealing by using *transitions* as elements transit in and out of the DOM. Svelte makes this easy with the *transition* directive. Let's apply transition to listing our todos in ToDoList.svelte.

First, import the *fade* function from *svelte/transition*:

Modify Bold Code
```
<script>
import {TodoStore} from '../stores';
import { Table, Button } from 'sveltestrap';
import {createEventDispatcher, onMount} from 'svelte';
import axios from 'axios';
import { fade } from 'svelte/transition';

...
```

Add it to the *<tr>* element in the table:

Modify Bold Code
```
...
    <tbody>
      {#each $TodoStore as todo (todo.id)}
        {#if !todo.complete}
          <tr transition:fade>
            <td>{todo.text}</td>
            <td>{todo.date}</td>
            ...
```

When you run your app now, the todos will be listed with a *fade* transition. Try out other transitions e.g. *scale, slide*.

115

Deployment

In this section, we will deploy our Svelte frontend to the Internet to share it with the world. We are going to use Vercel (vercel.com – fig.1) for our deployment.

Figure 1

Note: Before deploying on Vercel, note that you have to replace the fake API URL (e.g. localhost:4000/todos) in your Svelte project to the actual live API URL. Do this for all the API calls.

Deploying in Vercel is quite straightforward. You can follow the instructions at: https://vercel.com/guides/deploying-svelte-with-vercel

We will deploy using the Vercel CLI.

First, in your *sveltetodo* project folder, run:

Execute in Terminal

```
npm run build
```

This will create a build version of your app that we can deploy on the web. When the build is finished, you will be able to see a */public/build* folder with bundle.js in it.

116

Next, install the Vercel CLI by running in the Terminal:

Execute in Terminal

```
npm i -g vercel
```

Then, run 'vercel' to deploy. It will prompt you to log in with a Vercel account or sign up if you don't have one.

Answer the questions Vercel prompts you. Vercel will detect you are using Svelte, enable the correct settings for your deployment and generate a URL where you can access the page (fig. 2).

```
MacBook-Air:SvelteTodo user$ vercel
Vercel CLI 24.1.0
> > No existing credentials found. Please log in:
> Log in to Vercel email
> Enter your email address: limjunqu@gmail.com
We sent an email to limjunqu@gmail.com. Please follow the steps provided inside it and make sure the
iant Tortoise.
> Success! Email authentication complete for limjunqu@gmail.com
? Set up and deploy "~/Documents/svelte/SvelteTodo"? [Y/n] y
? Which scope do you want to deploy to? greglim81
? Link to existing project? [y/N] n
? What's your project's name? svelte-todo
? In which directory is your code located? ./
Auto-detected Project Settings (Svelte):
- Build Command: rollup -c
- Output Directory: public
- Development Command: rollup -c -w
? Want to override the settings? [y/N] y
? Which settings would you like to overwrite (select multiple)? None
   Linked to greglim81/svelte-todo (created .vercel and added it to .gitignore)
   Inspect: https://vercel.com/greglim81/svelte-todo/HX89LDNnq2LtAT8B8XFgLJBJ7Vmo [2s]
   Production: https://svelte-todo-murex.vercel.app [copied to clipboard] [23s]
   Deployed to production. Run `vercel --prod` to overwrite later (https://vercel.link/2F).
   To change the domain or build command, go to https://vercel.com/greglim81/svelte-todo/settings
```

Figure 2

Congratulations! Your application is deployed, meaning that your fully functioning Svelte app is live and running.

Summary

With this knowledge, you can move on and build more complicated enterprise-level fully functional Svelte applications of your own!

Hopefully, you have enjoyed this book and would like to learn more from me. I would love to get your feedback, learning what you liked and didn't for us to improve.

Please feel free to email me at support@i-ducate.com if you encounter any errors with your code, to get updated versions of this book or get the full source code.

If you didn't like the book, or if you feel that I should have covered certain additional topics, please email us to let us know. This book can only get better thanks to readers like you.

Thank you and all the best for your learning journey in Svelte!

ABOUT THE AUTHOR

Greg Lim is a technologist and author of several best-selling programming books. Greg has many years in teaching programming in tertiary institutions and he places special emphasis on learning by doing.

Contact Greg at support@i-ducate.com or on Twitter at @greglim81

ABOUT THE CO-AUTHOR

Daniel Correa is a researcher and has been a software developer for several years. Daniel has a Ph.D. in Computer Science. Currently, he is a professor at Universidad EAFIT in Colombia and writes programming books. He is interested in software architectures, frameworks (such as Laravel, Django, Express, Vue, React, Angular, and many more), web development, and clean code.

Daniel is very active on Twitter. He shares tips about software development. Contact Daniel on Twitter at @danielgarax

"Hecho en Medellín"

Made in United States
North Haven, CT
14 November 2023

44023210R00067